FOUNDATION

OF THE WORD

SECOND EDITION

Order this book online at www.trafford.com
or email orders@trafford.com

Most Trafford titles are also available at major online book retailers.

Print information available on the last page.

ISBN: 978-1-5536-9875-3 (sc)

Trafford rev. 06/08/2020

 www.trafford.com

North America & international
toll-free: 1 888 232 4444 (USA & Canada)
fax: 812 355 4082

INTRODUCTION

Do you find yourself confused and overwhelmed with Bible study? Do you ever wonder why you should study the Bible? Do you question if God has something to say to you through His Word? Do you wonder how you can learn more in less time? Do you think about how you can improve your relationship with God? This extraordinary book gives you an inspiring overview of the 66 books of the Bible. It will bring you unparalleled joy as you learn the major themes, the author of each book and the central message of the books along with scriptures. You will also learn fun techniques on how to recite all 66 books. This book is designed to invite new and seasoned Believers to obtain more knowledge of the word of God.

ABOUT THE AUTHOR

Dr. Dreamer L. Brown was born in Charleston, West Virginia to Deacon Aaron and Evangelist Clara M. Garrett. She was raised primarily in New York City until migrating to New Jersey in her adult years. She was Born Again and filled with the Holy Spirit as a child. At the age of fifteen, the Lord started using her with spiritual warfare gifts of deliverance. She is anointed and appointed by the Lord Jesus Christ for these last and evil days. Dr. Brown was ordained into the ministry in 1994. She was united in Holy Matrimony to her best friend, Overseer Willie M. Brown in 1980. She is the Pastor, along with her husband, of Christian Deliverance Ministry in Bordentown, New Jersey. She has been a teacher of the Word of God for nearly twenty years. She conducts revivals, educational workshops, seminars and conferences. She is also an anointed preacher of the Gospel who flows under the power of the Holy Spirit. Dr. Brown holds an honorary Doctorate in Theology from St. Paul's Bible Institute, honorary Doctorate in Divinity from World Christianship Ministries and a Business Management degree from New York University. She has worked in senior management positions for major corporations in the information technology field. She is a pastor, teacher, author, counselor, business woman, and a friend to many. To contact Dr. Brown, send an email to: willdream2@aol.com.

BOOK DEDICATION

First and foremost, I thank God for salvation, and being filled with His Holy Spirit for 26 years. Without the Lord's divine favor in my life, this work would not have been possible. I appreciate the students from Christian Deliverance Ministry who have taken this course and helped me enhance the material through our in-house course of study. Your prayers and support were essential in taking this project from vision to victory.

This book is dedicated to my husband, Overseer Willie M. Brown, who is my best friend next to Jesus. I cherish our relationship with the Lord and with one another. Your love and support has made it possible for me to pursue many dreams. Thank you for being my husband for 22 years, my best friend, and my spiritual covering. You are a great man of God and I encourage you to continue to remain steadfast in the Lord.

TABLE OF CONTENTS

TABLE OF CONTENTS

WHAT IS THE BIBLE?

The Bible is a "library of books" divided into two sections: the "Old Testament" and the "New Testament." In the Bible there are 66 books written by over 40 authors over a period of approximately 1600 years. The 40 human writers recorded the words inspired by God. Therefore, the Bible is the voice of God. The books of the Bible are **not** in chronological order, either according to the time they were written, or according to the events they describe.
The writers of the Bible were of many different occupations: Shepherds, Military leaders, Kings, Priests, Farmers, Tax collectors, Fishermen, Tent makers, Prophets, Apostles and a Physician.

WHY IS THE BIBLE DIVIDED INTO THE OLD AND NEW TESTAMENTS?
The translators divided the books into the Old and New Testaments many years after they were written. The Old Testament contains 39 books that were written in Hebrew with a few chapters written in Aramaic, while the New Testament contains 27 books that were written in Greek.

OLD TESTAMENT	39 BOOKS
NEW TESTAMENT	27 BOOKS **(3 X 9 OT = 27 New Testament)**

IS THERE A PERSONAL MESSAGE IN THE BIBLE FOR US?
There is a message of hope in the Bible called the Gospel, which means the good news or glad tidings of the coming Kingdom of God, and salvation from sin and death through the Lord Jesus Christ.

Overseer Willie M. Brown of Christian Deliverance Ministry in Bordentown, New Jersey often refers to the Bible as:

BIBLE: BASIC INSTRUCTIONS BEFORE LEAVING EARTH.

A BRIEF HISTORY OF THE ENGLISH BIBLE

The Bible was originally written on stone, clay tablets, leather, papyrus plant, scrolls, and fine quality animal skins from calves, sheep or goats. The Bible is now printed on paper in many versions and recorded in approximately 140 languages. The Bible is also on tape, compact discs, computer software, and on the internet.

From the early middle Ages until the Reformation of the sixteenth century, the Latin Vulgate was the official Bible of the Church. This was unfortunate, since only the highly educated could read Latin. Thus the Bible was a closed book to many. The later medieval period, however, saw the production of several partial translations into Old English (Anglo-Saxon). The first full translation of the Bible in English was the Middle English translation of John Wycliffe in **1380 A.D.**. Copies of it were made by hand because paper printing was not yet invented. Gutenburg invented the First Printing Press Company in the **1450's,** and one of the first books to ever be printed was the Bible. Still, it was not until the time of William Tyndale **(1525 A.D)** reformation that the Bible was translated into English from the original languages of Hebrew, Aramaic and Greek. William Tyndale, a scholar fluent in about eight languages, left England to work on the first English translation and from his work several English translations were eventually produced.

Any good Christian bookstore will present an array of Bibles to choose from. While nearly everyone have their favorite version, one of the most important habits of Bible study is to read and compare different translations in order to get a more complete understanding of what was originally written. In some areas, the older versions do a better job in staying with the original meaning of words, while in other places the newer versions make things clearer with the language of today. The King James Version of the Holy Bible written in 1611 A.D is a classic among the many English Bible translations. It has served generations of Christians for nearly 400 years. Even with several new translations available a great many people prefer to use this traditional favorite.

DISCUSSION QUESTIONS:

1. Is the Word of God an easy product to sell? Why or why not?

2. Knowing how great God's Word is, how much would you be willing to pay for a Bible?

3. Is Jesus your Lord? If you were arrested for being a Christian, would there be enough evidence to convict you? Or would they have to release you for lack of evidence? Think about this for a moment.

HISTORY - ENGLISH BIBLE

1380's	**John Wycliffe** was the first to translate the Bible into English from the Latin Language. Copies of it were made by hand because book printing was not yet invented. Because of his work of making a Bible available to the Englishmen, John Wycliffe was cast out of the church and his translation condemned.
1525	**William Tyndale** translated New Testament into English from Greek. Was translating Old Testament at the time of his death as a martyr. He was burned to death.
1535	**Coverdale** completed and published first complete Bible in English from Tyndale's work, Greek and Hebrew, and other sources.
1537	**Matthew's Bible**. A Complete English Bible from Tyndale's and Coverdale's work by John Rogers. Received royal sanction of King Henry VIII.
1539	**The Great Bible**. A revision by Coverdale of Matthew's Bible. Was placed in every church in England at the order of King Henry.
1560	**The Geneva Bible**. Produced by Protestant scholars in Geneva from the original languages and from Tyndale's work. First Bible to add verses to the chapters.
1568	**The Bishop's Bible**. A revision of the Great Bible. Was authorized by the Church of England as their official translation.
1610	**Douay Translation**. Roman Catholic translation from the Latin Vulgate of the Old and New Testaments so named because of where they were translated: the Old Testament at Douay in 1609-10 preceded by the translation of the New Testament at Rheims in 1582
1611	**The King James Version** (or authorized version). Commissioned by King James I of England and translated by a number of Bible scholars. A revision of the 1602 edition of the Bishop's Bible with the aid of the Hebrew and Greek texts and a dependence upon the work of William Tyndale.
1885	**The Revised Version**. A revision of the Authorized Version incorporating more recently discovered manuscripts and more modern language usage. By a group of British scholars and some American scholars.
1901	**The American Standard Version**. An American revision of the Authorized Version growing out of American scholars' participation in the Revised Version.
1903	**The New Testament in Modern Speech**. R. T. Weymouth's attempt to render Greek grammatical constructions carefully.
1924	**A New Translation of the Bible**. A formal, everyday, and sometimes Scottish translation by James Moffatt.
1927	**Centenary Translation of the New Testament**. Helen B. Montgomery's missionary heart produced a translation in the language of everyday life.
1937	**Williams New Testament**. By Charles B. Williams. A Baptist professor's attempt to translate into English the Greek verbs.
1938	**The Bible**: An American Translation. E. J. Goodspeed and J. M. Powis Smith produced

	the first modern American translation with the Apocrypha.
1952	**The Revised Standard Version**. Revision of the American Standard Version and the King James Version.
1955	**The Holy Bible**. Translated by Ronald Knox, a Roman Catholic, from the Latin Vulgate.
1958	**The New Testament in Modern English**. A free translation by J. B. Phillips originally done for his youth club.
1965	**The Amplified Bible**. A version by the Lockman Foundation suggesting various wordings throughout the text.
1966	**The Jerusalem Bible**. Originally translated into French by Roman Catholic scholars from the original languages.
1969	**The New Berkeley** (Modern Language) Bible. A revision of the Berkeley Version of 1959 with attached notes.
1970	**The New English Bible**. A translation with literary quality but some idiosyncratic language. Translated by representatives of Britain's major churches and Bible societies and based on the most recent textual evidence.
1970	**The New American Bible**. A new translation by Roman Catholic scholars from the original languages.
1971	**The New American Standard Bible**. A revision by the Lockman Foundation of the American Standard Version of 1901 with the goal of maintaining literal translation.
1971	**The Living Bible**. A conservative American paraphrase by Kenneth N. Taylor originally for his children (begun in 1962).
1976	**The Good News Bible** A translation by the American Bible Society into English.
1978	**The New International Version**. A readable translation by evangelical scholars incorporating the most recent textual evidence.
1982	**The New King James Version**. A modernization of the King James Version of 1611. Based on the original language texts available to the King James Version translators.
1987	**The New Century Version**. A translation committee's update of the International Children's Bible.
1989	**The New Revised Standard Version**. A translation committee's update of the Revised Standard Version.
1989	**The Revised English Bible**. A British committee's update of the New English Bible maintaining literary quality but avoiding idiosyncratic language.
1991	**The Contemporary English Version** (New Testament). A simplified text originally conceived for children and produced by the American Bible Society.
1995	**God's Word** looks and reads like contemporary American literature. It uses natural grammar, follows standard punctuation and capitalization rules.
1996	**New Living Translation** is a translation to overcome some of the barriers of history, culture, and language that have kept people from reading and understanding God's Word.

STUDYING THE BIBLE

You may wish to consider getting a "Study Bible" (rather than a "regular Bible"). A Study Bible adds notes to the text of a regular Bible *(usually at the bottom of each page)* that should improve your understanding of the scriptures. The "Bible content" of a regular Bible and a Study Bible are the same. However, the Study Bible will add notes, maps, dictionaries, commentaries, etc. There are many different Study Bibles. Look around and pick one that you prefer. When choosing your Bible think about other ways it can help you understand the scriptures. Ideally, choose a Bible with cross references that will help you find quotations and parallel passages. Some Bibles even have a commentary and a small concordance in the back, where you can look up particular words.

The BIBLE is essentially a library of 66 books. The first book of the Bible, Genesis, is a great foundation, but it is not necessarily a good starting place for a "beginner." Start with the book of **Mark** or one of the other Gospel books (Matthew, Luke or John). Mark is the second of the four Biblical "biographies" of Jesus and quickly moves through the manifestation of Jesus earthly life. Do not allow some words or terms to discourage you. You just started reading the Bible and may not understand everything, but your understanding will improve over time. The Gospel books are easier to understand than starting in the Old Testament.

After reading your first Gospel book (Matthew, Mark, Luke or John), read the book called **"Acts,"** the fifth book in the New Testament. It describes the adventures of a number of the people who walked the earth with Jesus. After reading Acts, read the next book in the Bible, called **"Romans."** You will notice that this book is quite different from the first two you read, yet it will "tie in" what the other two books covered. Then read the book of **Genesis**, the first book in the Bible. After you complete these first four books, read a book of your choice in the New Testament. Then go back to the Old Testament and read a book of your choice there. Keep going back and forth. Studying the Bible requires discipline and is essential for your spiritual growth.

Store a Bible for easy access in rooms within your home that are most occupied. Having a Bible within reach should inspire you to study God's word more. You may want to also consider loading the Bible on your computer or listening to Bible CD's or cassettes.

BIBLE KEY-TERMS

CONCORDANCE

A concordance is an alphabetical index of the words found in one or more versions of the Bible. It is a text finder that enables the reader to locate a particular verse by looking up a key word.

TOPICAL INDEX

A topical Bible lists references to ideas and themes, regardless of whether the actual words are mentioned. A topical Bible will give references in the Bible for you to look up regarding the topic, and you can use it with any translation.

BIBLE DICTIONARY

A Bible Dictionary is similar to a regular dictionary but provides more information on Christian terms. Some Bible dictionaries include maps, illustrations, history and a concordance.

BIBLE HANDBOOK

A Bible Handbook is similar to a Bible dictionary. The main difference is that a Bible dictionary has short articles arranged alphabetically, while a Bible handbook provides a brief running commentary of each of the books of the Bible. It contains maps, historical backgrounds, archaeological background, tables of weights and measures, lists of kings and genealogies and other information.

BIBLE ENCYCLOPEDIA

Bible encyclopedias are multi volume sets of articles about people, places, and subjects arranged in alphabetical order. It is similar to a Bible Dictionary but with more information.

HOW TO USE A COMMENTARY

A Bible commentary is a book written by an author about the different books in the Bible. It explains different passages but expresses the doctrinal beliefs of the author. The commentary remarks are added by human writers as study helps to the reader. Don't take the commentary as the Gospel and please don't read the commentary instead of the Bible. Although commentaries are from authors that have carefully and prayerfully sought revelation of the Word, the writer is giving you their interpretation of the scripture. Yet, you must read the Word for yourself. Commentaries are good for Bible study, but they must be used properly. Consult them only after you have carefully studied the scripture yourself. After you have done your best to understand a passage, then read the commentary. If you use the commentary before you have read the Word, you may take away from what the Lord wants to reveal to you.

What will the effective use of good commentaries do for you as you study the Bible? Here are some results you might expect.

1. Sometimes they will confirm your understanding of the passage. When you find that all of the commentaries interpret the scriptures essentially the same way you do, you can be confident that you are on target in your conclusions. This should confirm you have understanding of the Word.

2. Sometimes they will refine your understanding of the passage. The commentators may present insights that didn't come to your mind, therefore enriching your understanding of the scripture. Similarly, when we hear the preached word of God, we often gain new insight. A good commentary is beneficial in opening our minds to thoughts of a passage that we may otherwise have neglected or not noticed.

3. Sometimes they will lead you to revaluate your interpretations. Occasionally you will find that the commentaries present interpretation of the Word contrasting your own interpretation. After prayer and careful thought, you may come to understand that the scripture had a different meaning from what you first believed.

4. Sometimes they will show you that your understanding of the passage was entirely wrong. Reading the commentaries may give you information that will make you realize that you have totally misunderstood certain Bible verses. Pray and ask the Holy Spirit to open up your understanding of the Word.

BASIC CHARACTER OF BIBLE STUDY

Bible study is the process by which we dive deeply into the text of the Bible in order to better understand what has been written. When you prepare to study the Bible, **always begin with Prayer** asking God to open up your understanding of His Word.

1. OBSERVATION: WHAT DOES IT SAY?

Don't add your own interpretation at this stage, just observe the facts.

- What does it say?
- Who is involved?
- What are they doing?
- Where are they?
- When did this happen?

2. INTERPRETATION: WHAT DOES IT MEAN?

Interpretation of the Bible verses should never be taken out of context. Prayerfully and carefully study the word.

- Who is the author?
- To whom is it written?
- What is the literary and cultural context of the passage?
- What does it mean? Prayerfully meditate on the contents.
- How does it compare with other passages on the same subject?

3. APPLICATION: HOW IT APPLIES?

Application of the Bible verses should take place after you have studied the scriptures.

- What does it mean to me?
- What does the Holy Spirit want me to apply to my life?

UNDERSTANDING BIBLICAL DATES
"BC" and "AD"

A basic historical concept that needs to be emphasized is the distinction between dates "B.C" and "A.D"—and what these abbreviations stand for. Hundreds of years after the time Jesus lived on the earth, some scholars decided to use the year of His birth as the **"focal"** point of history. This method of describing time is almost universal now.

All dates **BEFORE** his birth would be considered "B.C"—**Before Christ**. All dates **AFTER** His birth would be "A.D"—which is an abbreviation of the Latin phrase **Anno Domini**. The word "Anno" refers to the concept of "year" and thus shows up as a source for such English words as "annual" and "anniversary." The word "Domini" refers to the concept of "Lord" and shows up as a source for such English words as "dominate" and "dominion". Thus Anno Domini means **"The Year of Our Lord"**, referring to the Lordship of Jesus.

There are groups, in recent years, which have reacted unfavorably to the notion that they should use a **"Christian"** definition of time. Realizing that they cannot possibly get the whole world to accept some totally new method of dating at this point in history, they have dealt with the issue by a symbolic change of the abbreviations used. Some religious groups now use B.C.E and C.E to replace B.C. and A.D.

OTHER DATE ABBREVIATIONS
"BCE" AND "CE"

B.C.E stands for **"Before the Common Era"**. Used instead of B.C (Before Christ) because some do not believe that dates should be centered on Christ. This abbreviation has come to replace the previously used B.C. ("Before Christ"), and covers the same period of history.

C.E stands for **"Common Era"**, meaning the "commonly used system" of dating. Some use C.E instead of A.D., because A.D. means "The Year of our Lord," and some religions do not believe that Jesus is Lord. The Common Era covers the same time period from Christ's birth to the present day.

BOOKS OF THE BIBLE

OLD TESTAMENT

Genesis
Exodus
Leviticus
Numbers
Deuteronomy
Joshua
Judges
Ruth
1 Samuel
2 Samuel
1 Kings
2 Kings
1 Chronicles
2 Chronicles
Ezra
Nehemiah
Esther
Job
Psalms
Proverbs
Ecclesiastes
Song of Solomon
Isaiah
Jeremiah
Lamentations
Ezekiel
Daniel
Hosea
Joel
Amos
Obadiah
Jonah
Micah
Nahum
Habakkuk
Zephaniah
Haggai
Zechariah
Malachi

NEW TESTAMENT

Matthew
Mark
Luke
John
Acts
Romans
1 Corinthians
2 Corinthians
Galatians
Ephesians
Philippians
Colossians
1 Thessalonians
2 Thessalonians
1 Timothy
2 Timothy
Titus
Philemon
Hebrews
James
1 Peter
2 Peter
1 John
2 John
3 John
Jude
Revelation

FUN LEARNING TECHNIQUES BENEFICIAL FOR TEAM BUILDING

The secret to learning the books of the Bible is **REPETITION** - but at the same time trying to maintain variety, so that it doesn't become boring. It's important to reinforce the teaching using games and quizzes. This gives the opportunity to introduce some "fun" elements that will encourage learning. Use a variety of these to keep the fun going for weeks at a time. These exercises may also be used for team building with group studies.

WORD ASSOCIATION: We remember things by association. Every piece of information in our memory is connected to other pieces in some way or another. With a little creativity you can take the first letter of each word and make a word or a sentence. **Example: God Expects Love Night & Day** (Represents the first letter of the first 5 books of the Bible.)

FIND THE MISSING BOOK: Prepare a series of transparencies with the books listed in order, but with one missing (don't have a gap where the missing book should be). Show a series of these and see if you could identify the missing book. (Samples included)

REGULAR QUIZ QUESTIONS: If you are running a quiz, introduce a few questions such as "which book comes before Romans?" or "which book comes after Hebrews?" (Samples included)

BIBLE NAMES SCRAMBLE: Scramble the books of the Bible with cards made on your computer and have your students try to put them back in order. The cards may be created with business cards purchased from your local office supplier.

BOOK RACE: A very popular game is putting all 66 books of the Bible cards face down on the floor. Form two teams, assigning one team the Old Testament and the other team the New Testament. The object is to retrieve all the cards for the appropriate testament and put them in correct order on a table. Each team is timed. Then the game is played again working with the opposite testament. The two times are added together to determine a winner. Students will have a great time getting on the floor trying to find the right cards, and then racing to the finish.

BEAT THE RECORD: Get a stopwatch, and ask somebody who has learned the books to come out and see how quickly they can say them correctly. Then ask others to come out and try to do it in a faster time.

REVERSE RECITALS: See if you can learn to recite all 66 Bible books backwards. This is a lot of fun for group studies.

BIBLE BOOK TEAM GAME: Divide the group into two equal teams. Choose one team to go first; they will name the first book of the Bible. If they are correct they hand the Bible to the other team. The next team names the second book of the Bible, if they name the book correctly, they hand the Bible back to the first team. This continues until the groups have named all the books of the Bible or until one of the teams can not name the next book. If a team can not name the next book, the opposing team must be able to name it in order to win. When the groups get really good at it, you can have them spell the books of the Bible as they take turns reciting them in order. Groups on the same team can help each other.

LINE UP: Put the 6 category cards face up on a table and deal the 66 Bible cards to your students. The player who has Genesis starts by placing it next to the "Law" category. If the same player has Exodus, he/she can also play that card by placing it half way over the Genesis card and so on. For categories that have both Old Testament and New Testament books, such as "prophecy, cards can be placed in both directions, but always starting with the first book of the category, then in proper order. A player can only start a category on the first card played during their turn, but can build on a category until they no longer can. Play continues clockwise. The first player to place all of his/her cards down on the table wins, but the other players continue until all the books are placed in the proper order.

BIBLE BOX GAME: Write each of the books of the Bible on a medium size box. Select one team for the Old Testament and the other for the New Testament. Each team must move the boxes in order from one side of the room to the other. Time how long it takes each team to complete the stacking of their books in order and by categories. Rotate the teams (old to new, etc.) The team with the highest combined score for the Old and New Testament wins the game.

WORD SEARCH: A word search can help students remember the spelling of the Bible books. (Samples included)

STANDING FOR KNOWLEDGE: Have everyone stand. Start with Genesis (or Matthew if you are doing the New Testament) and have everybody say each book in order all together. If someone can't say the next book, they must sit down. For a variation, make a circle and say the books in order with the next person saying the next book. Again, if you get to a person that doesn't know the book, they must sit down until one winner is left standing.

BIBLE BOOK SONGS: Some students enjoy singing the books of the Bible to help them memorize it. There are some Bible Book CD's you may purchase at your local Christian bookstore.

SCRIPTURE FUN LEARNING TECHNIQUES

SCRIPTURE MEMORY: When teaching Scripture memory verses during class time you will want to let the students repeat the verse at least ten times to help them remember it. But remember always do it in a fun, exciting way. Regardless of the age group, learning the Bible could be fun.

FIRST FOUR STEPS TO MEMORIZATION: Let's use "Hebrews 4:12: For the word of God is quick, and powerful, and sharper than any two edged sword, piercing even to the dividing asunder of soul and spirit, and of the joints and marrow, and is a discerner of the thoughts and intents of the heart." Now let's learn how to memorize this scripture.

STEP 1: LOCATION: The first step is to memorize the **location**, not the verse. The reason for this is if you forget the verse, but you've memorized the location, you can always go look it up. First, memorize the location: "**Hebrews 4:12**."

> Say Hebrews 4:12 repeatedly. Don't worry about what it says at first, just memorize the location. Say Hebrews 4:12 enough times that it feels natural and comfortable when you say it.

STEP 2: GET THE GENERAL IDEA: The second step is to learn the general idea of what the verse is. In this case it is very simple. Say: Hebrews 4:12 speaks of God's word.

STEP 3: REPEATING THE VERSE: Take a few words at a time and continue to expand your words as you learn to memorize. Say: **Hebrews 4:12:** For the word of God is quick, and powerful. Say this over and over again, about ten times. Now add more words to your memory. Say: **Hebrews 4:12:** For the word of God is quick, and powerful, and sharper than any two edged sword. Say this over and over again, about ten times. Now add more words to your memory. Say: **Hebrews 4:12:** For the word of God is quick, and powerful and sharper than any two edged sword piercing even to the dividing asunder of soul and spirit, and of the joints and marrow, and is a discerner of the thoughts and intents of the heart. In no time, you will have the verse memorized. Continue to take a few words at a time and continue to expand your words as you memorize.

STEP 4: INDEX CARDS: The fourth step is to make up index cards. You can purchase cards to print on your computer from any office supply store or simply write on index cards the Bible verses you want to remember. Put the cards in your pocket or purse, and carry it with you everywhere you go. When you forget a verse or its location simply pull out the card and refresh your memory.

SCRIPTURE
FUN LEARNING TECHNIQUES

ERASE-A-WORD: Write the verse on a blackboard or whiteboard. Each time the verse is repeated choose a student to erase another word until all are gone and the students can say the verse without seeing it. If it is a long verse try letting the first student erase one word, the second two, the third three and so on.

CLAP AND GUESS: After repeating the verse several times to familiarize your students with it, choose one student to come and stand with his back towards the class. Have another student come and point to a single word in the verse on your verse visual without saying the word. The class now says the verse clapping on, instead of saying, the chosen word. The student at the front then must guess which word was clapped on. Second chances are, of course, permitted since the objective is really that the student would repeat the verse enough times to remember it.

TEACHING WITH MUSIC: Learning through music is very effective because music makes learning more fun and easier to remember. Can you recall the ingredients of a **Big Mac**? "Two all beef patties, special sauce.."Do you still sing the **ABC's** to remember what comes after 'K'? Try using song beats to remember the Scriptures.

PLAN A GRADUATION DAY: Plan a short ceremony with your class members who are able to recite the 66 books of the Bible and have obtained a general foundation of the Bible. Each Graduate will receive a course completion certificate. Ask others to come out and celebrate with your students.

FIVE DIVISIONS OF OLD TESTAMENT

Now let's start our study in the Old Testament which has 39 books. Learn the divisions and names of the Old Testament books in order.

There are five divisions and you may learn them by associating them with **THE FIVE FINGERS**.

LAW	**05 BOOKS**
HISTORY	**12 BOOKS**
POETRY	**05 BOOKS**
MAJOR PROPHETS	**05 BOOKS**
MINOR PROPHETS	**12 BOOKS**

APPLICATION

Write a sentence or song using the first letters of each section to help you memorize the five sections of the Old Testament.

THE LAW (TORAH) - 05 BOOKS

The first five books of the Old Testament are called the Pentateuch, the Torah or the Law according to Jewish and Christian traditions. The Pentateuch, or what later became known as the Torah or 'books of Law', was regarded as the most authoritative and highly inspired of all the Old Testament writings. This section was called the "Law" because its focus is the covenant law revealed to Moses on Mount Sinai (Exodus 20). The Law contains the books of Moses, which present the beginnings of the world and of the covenant people Israel.

GENESIS   AUTHOR: MOSES

EXODUS   AUTHOR: MOSES

LEVITICUS   AUTHOR: MOSES

NUMBERS   AUTHOR: MOSES

DEUTERONOMY   AUTHOR: MOSES

GENESIS

Genesis is a name taken from the Greek, and signifies the book of generation or beginnings. Genesis explains how everything began. In fact, the Bible is the only book that accurately does so. Genesis explains how God created the universe, including all the animals and humans. It describes the temptation of Adam and Eve in the Garden of Eden. It includes a good narrative of human history up to the time of the Jewish exile in Egypt.

AUTHOR: Moses

APPROXIMATE DATE: 1450 and 1410 B.C.

THEME: Blessings and Covenant. Genesis is the book of beginnings.

MAJOR CONTENTS
1. Creation of the universe (1:1 - 2:4)
2. Life in the Garden of Eden (2:5 - 3:24)
3. Adam's sin and its consequences (3:1-5:32)
4. Pre-flood civilization (4:1 - 6:4)
5. Cain and Abel (4:1-16)
6. Man who lived to be 969 years old (5:27)
7. The Noachian flood and new earth (6:5 - 9:29)
8. The division of the nations (10:1 - 11:26)
9. The Tower of Babel (11)
10. Abraham's obedience (12:1-19)
11. Sodom and Gomorrah (19)
12. Attempted sacrifice of Isaac (22:1-19)
13. The lives of the patriarchs (11:27 - 50:26)
14. Man used a stone for a pillow (28:11)

DAYS OF CREATION	
First Day	Light (so there was light and darkness)
Second Day	Sky (Heaven) and water (waters separated)
Third Day	Land and seas (waters gathered); Vegetation
Fourth Day	Sun, moon, and the stars (to govern the day and the night and to mark seasons, days, and years)
Fifth Day	Fish and the birds (to fill the waters and the sky)
Sixth Day	Animals (to fill the earth) Man and woman (to care for the earth and fellowship with God)
Seventh Day	God rested and declared all He had made was good

SCRIPTURE MEMORIZATION

Gen 1:1: In the beginning God created the_____ and the _____ .

Gen 1:27: So God created man in _____ _____ _____, in the image of God created he him; _____ and _____created he them.

Gen 1:29: What did the first humans eat? _____

Gen 2:9: Name the two special trees in the Garden of Eden.

_____

Gen 2:17: Which tree in the garden was man not to eat from? _____

Gen 4:1-16: What was the name of Cain's brother and why did Cain kill him?

_____

Gen 5:27: And all the days of _____ were nine hundred sixty and nine years: and he died.

Gen 9:28: Look up and learn how many years did Noah live after the flood? _____

Gen 11:9: At what place did God create the different languages? _____

Gen 11:31: How was Lot related to Abraham? _____

Gen 15:13: Look up and learn how many years were the Israelites in bondage as slaves?

_____

Gen 19:26: Whose wife turned into a pillar of salt? _____

Gen 22:14: What did Abraham name the place he was going to sacrifice Isaac at? What does this name mean? _____

Gen 50:20: But as for you, ye thought _____ against me; but God meant it unto _____, to bring to pass, as it is this day, to _____ much people alive.

Gen 50:26: Who does the Bible record as being the first person embalmed and placed in a coffin? _____

22

EVENTS OF THE FLOOD

		EVENTS	SCRIPTURE
Waiting in the ark for 7 days (7:7, 10)	1	Noah entered the ark	Genesis 7:7-9
	2	7 days later: The rain began to fall	Genesis 7:10-11
Water continued for 150 days (7:24)	3	40 days later: Heavy rains stopped	Genesis 7:12
	4	110 days later: Prevailing waters receded and the ark rested on an Ararat mountain	Genesis 7:24 Genesis 8:4
Water receded in 150 days (8:3)	5	74 days later: Tops of mountains became visible	Genesis 8:5
	6	40 days later: Raven sent out, and a dove sent out and returned	Genesis 8:6-9
	7	7 days later: Dove sent out again and returned with a leaf	Genesis 8:10
	8	7 days later: Dove sent out a third time and did not return	Genesis 8:12
	9	22 days later: Water receded	Genesis 8:3
Earth dried in 70 days	10	Noah saw the dry land	Genesis 8:13
	11	Land was completely dry	Genesis 8:14-19
377 days in the ark			

God gave a **rainbow** to remind of His covenant with Noah to never again destroy the earth by flooding (Genesis 9:8-17).

Noah lived after the flood three hundred and fifty years (Genesis 9:28-29).

LIFE OF ABRAHAM

EVENTS	OLD TESTAMENT SCRIPTURE	NEW TESTAMENT SCRIPTURE
The birth of Abram	Genesis 11:26	
God's call of Abram to be the father of nations	Genesis 12:1-3	Hebrews 11:8
Abram entry into Canaan	Genesis 12:4-9	
Abram in Egypt	Genesis 12:10-20	
Lot separates from Abram	Genesis 13:1-18	
Abram rescues Lot	Genesis 14:1-17	
Abram pays tithes to Melchizedek	Genesis 14:18-24	Hebrews 7:1-10
God's covenant with Abraham	Genesis 15:1-21	Romans 4:1-25 Galatians 3:6-25 Hebrews 6:13-20
The birth of Ishmael by handmaid	Genesis 16:1-16	
Abraham promised a son with his wife, Sarah	Genesis 17:1-27	Romans 4:18-25 Hebrews 11:11-12
Abraham intercedes for Sodom	Genesis 18:16-33	
Lot saved and Sodom destroyed	Genesis 19:1-38	
The birth of promised son, Isaac	Genesis 21:1-7	
Hagar and Ishmael sent away	Genesis 21:8-21	Galatians 4:21-31
Abraham challenged to offer his beloved son Isaac as a sacrifice	Genesis 22:1-19	Hebrews 11:17-19 James 2:20-24
The death of Abraham's wife, Sarah	Genesis 23:1-20	
The death of Abraham	Genesis 25:1-11	

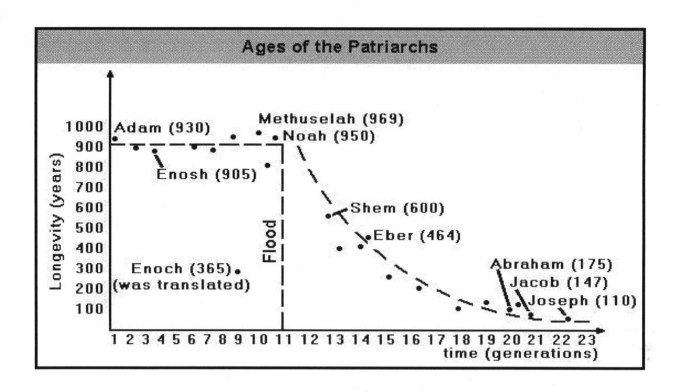

THE TWELVE TRIBES
OF ISRAEL

The history of Israel begins with the stories of the Patriarchs (Abraham, Isaac, Jacob, and Joseph). Jacob, the son of Isaac who was the son of Abraham, was born in Canaan. The struggle between Jacob and Esau began right from their conception. Although twins, Jacob and Esau were very different in appearance and personality and each was a favorite of one parent. Esau the firstborn turned out to be Isaac's favorite and Jacob was Rebecca's favorite. After Jacob wrestled with the angel, God changed Jacob's name to "Israel." From Jacob the nation of Israel was birthed.

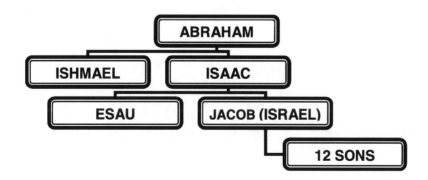

Jacob was a shrewd and dishonest business man who tricked his brother Esau out of his birthright and his paternal blessing (Gen. 25:29-34; 27:1-41). One of the most well-known stories of the Bible is Jacob's "stairway to heaven" dream (Gen. 28:10-22). The dream had a prophetic meaning - Jesus Christ had humanly descended from Abraham, Isaac and Jacob. He is our stairway to Heaven that will provide us with the way to get from earth to Heaven. The foot on earth is His human nature; the top in Heaven is His divine nature. As Jacob fled from the wrath of his brother, Esau, to his uncle, Laban's house, he was tricked by his uncle into working for him for 14 years in exchange for his desired wife. First, Jacob agreed to work seven years to marry the younger beautiful sister Rachel, but when the time was completed, Laban did a honeymoon switch. Instead of Jacob sleeping with Rachel, he found himself in bed with her older sister Leah (Gen. 29:16-30). When Jacob protested, Laban offered Rachel for another seven years of work. The same skills of deceit and dishonesty that Jacob showed towards his brother Esau was returned to him by his uncle Laban. As the saying goes "What goes around, comes around" or "You reap what you sow." After many years of working for his uncle, Jacob returned to his homeland and sought reconciliation with his brother Esau. Jacob had 2 wives, Rachel and Leah and 2 concubines, Bilhah and Zilpah. Between these four women, Jacob fathered 12 sons and one daughter named Dinah. Jacob's 12 sons were the ancestors of the 12 tribes of Israel. Whenever the Bible speaks of the whole house of Israel, it is referring to the descendants of these twelve men. Israel's favorite son, Joseph, was sold into slavery in Egypt by his 10 older brothers. While in Egypt, he becomes second only to Pharaoh, and in that office is given a wife. By her, he has two sons, Manasseh and Ephraim. Israel will treat Joseph's two sons, Manasseh and Ephraim, as his very own.

CHILDREN OF JACOB
12 SONS – 1 DAUGHTER

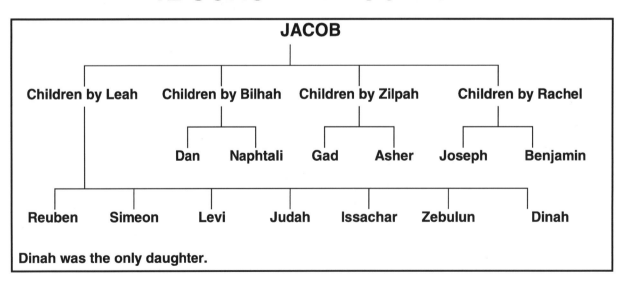

JOSEPH was the 11th son of Jacob and the first son of Jacob's favorite wife, Rachel. Joseph's favored status and his coat of many colors, a gift from his father, caused his brothers to be jealous of him, and they staged his "death." At an early age, Joseph was receiving revelations and dreams and dreamed his brothers would all someday bow down to him. The 10 brothers got so mad that they sold him to a caravan going to Egypt and then pretended he was dead. Joseph was actually taken to Egypt, where his ability to interpret dreams brought him into favor with Pharaoh. As time progressed, his brothers needed Joseph and instead of showing resentment towards them, he showed his brothers tremendous love. In Genesis 50:20 he said: "But as for you, ye thought evil against me; but God meant it unto good, to bring to pass, as it is this day, to save much people alive." Joseph became a high Egyptian official and from Joseph came two tribes named after his sons Ephraim and Manasseh.

JUDAH was Jacob's fourth son, of Leah. Judah means "Praise the Lord." Using its standard of the lion recognized universally as a symbol of courage, this tribe became the most powerful and significantly important leader for the House of Israel.

ISSACHAR was Jacob's fifth son, of Leah. The descendants of Issachar were inclined to sitting in the tent to learn from the Torah.

BENJAMIN was Jacob's twelfth son, of Rachel. Benjamin was the youngest son of Jacob and the name of the smallest of Israel's twelve tribes. Because Jacob's favorite wife, Rachel, died after Benjamin's birth, he was especially dear to his father and to his full brother, Joseph. The tribe of Benjamin became noted for brotherly love and strengthening the foundations of the Temple. The first King of Israel, Saul, was a descendant of this tribe.

REUBEN was Jacob's first born son, of Leah, firstborn of the twelve. Reuben, from the time of his conception, was involved with deceptions as his father Jacob was. He was known for committing an act of sexual immorality with Jacob's concubine Bilhah (Genesis 35:22).

LEVI was Jacob's third son, of Leah. Moses, Aaron and Miriam were Levi's great grandchildren. Their tribe was that of the priesthood carrying out the difficult task of carrying the tabernacle and its vessels throughout the wanderings in the desert. They encamped in the center of all the tribes surrounding the tabernacle and in such a way, represented the heart of the nation, unifying and synthesizing all of Israel –the musicians, teachers of Torah and leaders of prayer and meditation. The Levites were set apart for the secondary duties of the sanctuary service.

NAPHTALI was Jacob's sixth son, of Bilhah.

MANASSEH was actually Joseph's eldest son, but later recognized as a separate tribe in Genesis 48:5. Manasseh and Ephraim were counted instead of Joseph and Levi.

EPHRAIM was actually Joseph' second son, but later recognized as a separate tribe in Genesis 48:5. Manasseh and Ephraim counted instead of Joseph and Levi.

GAD was Jacob's seventh son, of Zilpah. Gad's allotment was half of Gilead.

ASHER was Jacob's eighth son, of Zilpah. Out of Asher his bread shall be fat and he shall yield royal dainties. In Genesis 49:20 the tribe of Asher ultimately became known as nurturers supplying bounteous food for the House of Israel. They became noted for their gracious nobility, untouched by corruption and endowed with fulfilling everyone's needs.

SIMEON was Jacob's second son, of Leah "And Jacob said to Simeon and Levi, Ye have troubled me to make me to stink among the inhabitants of the land, among the Canaanites and the Perizzites: and I being few in number, they shall gather themselves together against me, and slay me; and I shall be destroyed, I and my house. And they said, Should he deal with our sister as with a harlot? (Genesis 34:30-31)."

DAN was Jacob's ninth son, of Bilhah. Dan was seldom mentioned in the Bible.

ZEBULON OR ZEBULUN was Jacob's tenth son, of Leah. He was seldom mentioned in the Bible.

All 12 of Jacob's sons became the ancestors of the tribes of Israel, and the ones for whom the tribes were named. After the Israelites entered and took control of the land promised to them by God, it was divided into territories for each of the tribes. This occurred during the time of Joshua (Joshua 14-21). Each tribe occupied a separate territory (except the tribe of Levi, which was set apart to serve in the Holy Temple). With their consecration to the Lord's service, the Levites were allotted no territorial inheritance of their own at the division of the land because the Levites formed the priesthood. Joseph had two sons, Ephraim and Manasseh; these became the names of two independent tribes to replace the tribe of Joseph. Israel was once a very united country. However, eventually the Kingdom of Israel was divided by political and religious differences into two kingdoms. Ten tribes joined together as the northern kingdom, which retained the title of Israel. The other two tribes (Judah and Benjamin) formed the southern kingdom known as the tribe of Judah, and Jerusalem was the capital city.

SEPARATION OF TRIBES

NORTHERN TRIBE

The tribe of Dan and its related tribes Asher and Naphtali were positioned on the north side. The subtotal of the men of war in these three tribes was 157,600. In the line of march, they were the last group to move out of the camp.

DAN	62,700
ASHER	41,500
NAPHTALI	53,400
TOTAL NORTH	**157,600**

WESTERN TRIBE

Positioned on the west side were the tribe of Ephraim and its related tribes Manasseh and Benjamin. The subtotal of the men of war in these three tribes was 108,100. In the line of march, they were the third group to move out.

EPHRAIM	40,500
MANASSEH	32,200
BENJAMIN	35,400
TOTAL WEST	**108,100**

EASTERN TRIBE

Positioned on the east side were the tribe of Judah, with its related tribes Issachar and Zebulun. The subtotal of the men of war in these three tribes was 186,400. They were the first group to move out.

JUDAH	74,600
ISSACHAR	54,400
ZEBULUN	57,400
TOTAL EAST	**186,400**

SOUTHERN TRIBE

Positioned on the south side were the tribe of Reuben and its related tribes Simeon and Gad. The subtotal of the men of war in these three tribes was 151,450. They set out second, after the tribes allied with Judah.

REUBEN	46,500
SIMEON	59,300
GAD	45,650
TOTAL SOUTH	**151,450**

EXODUS

The book of Exodus begins after the Hebrews had been in Egypt for around 400 years. Exodus signifies "the departure;" the chief event therein recorded is the departure of Israel from Egypt and Egyptian bondage; it plainly points out the fulfilling of several promises and prophecies to Abraham respecting his seed, and shadows forth the state of the church, in the wilderness of this world, until her arrival at the heavenly Canaan, an eternal rest. This book includes the famous climax of the Jewish escape, the crossing of the Red Sea. The book then describes the people's wanderings and rebellious nature, and how the Ten Commandments came to be. The book concludes with a detailed description of the making of the first temple of worship.

AUTHOR: Moses

APPROXIMATE DATE: 1445 – 1405 B.C.

THEME: The Exile and Redemption

MAJOR CONTENTS
1. The emergence of Moses (1-6)
2. The Burning Bush (3:1-22)
3. Plagues, Passover, and the Exodus (7:1 – 15:21)
4. Red Sea experience (14:15-30)
5. Testing in the wilderness (15:22 – 18:27)
6. Law and covenant (19-24)
7. The Ten Commandments (20:1-17)
8. The Golden Calf (32:1-29)
9. Tabernacle and covenant renewal (25-40)

SCRIPTURE MEMORIZATION

Exo 3:7: And the Lord said, I have _____ seen the _____ of my people which are in Egypt, and have heard their cry by reason of their _____; for I know their _____.

Exo 13:22: What guided the Israelites **at night** in the desert? _____

Exo 13:22: What guided the Israelites **by day** in the desert? _____

Exo 14:14: The Lord shall _____ for you, and ye shall hold your _____.

Exo 32:33: And the Lord said unto _____, whosoever hath _____ against me, him will I _____ out of my book.

TEN COMMANDMENTS QUIZ

Yes	No	Check **YES** or **NO** to indicate which phrases are apart of the Ten Commandments given to Moses. ## (EXODUS 20:1-17 OR DEUTERONOMY 5)
		01. You shall not steal
		02. You shall not smoke
		03. Honor your father and your mother
		04. You shall not make for yourself an idol or bow down to them
		05. You shall not lie
		06. Do to others as you would have them do to you
		07. You shall not misuse the name of the Lord
		08. You must obey God rather than man
		09. You shall not give false testimony against your neighbor
		10. You shall not murder
		11. In God we trust
		12. You shall have no other gods before me
		13. Remember the Sabbath day by keeping it holy
		14. Be kind to the poor
		15. You shall not commit adultery
		16. You shall not covet your neighbor's property

TEN PLAGUES

THE FIRST PLAGUE   **EXODUS 7:14-24**

All of the river waters in Egypt turned into blood. Then all of the fish of the river died, causing an unpleasant smell. The first plague seemed to have no effect on Pharaoh (Exodus 7:23). His magicians imitated the turning of water to blood.

THE SECOND PLAGUE   **EXODUS 8:1-15**

Frogs miraculously multiplied in number and infested the land. Even people's houses had frogs inside them. The second plague caught Pharaoh's attention (Exodus 8:8).

THE THIRD PLAGUE   **EXODUS 8:16-19**

Vast swarms of gnats tormented people and animals. The third plague was lice on man and beast. The magicians could not imitate it. Rather they declared "This is the finger of God."

THE FOURTH PLAGUE   **EXODUS 8:20-32**

Vast swarms of flies filled the land and spreading disease.

THE FIFTH PLAGUE   **EXODUS 9:1-7**

Disease on the livestock – horses, donkeys, camels, cattle, sheep and goats – but those of the Israelites were unharmed. Pharaoh's heart was still hardened.

THE SIXTH PLAGUE   **EXODUS 9:8-12**

Festering boils on people and animals through out the land.

THE SEVENTH PLAGUE   **EXODUS 9:13-35**

Powerful hail storms that destroyed the standing crops. The hail stones were so big that people and animals caught outside in the storm were killed.

THE EIGHTH PLAGUE   **EXODUS 10: 1-20**

Locusts covered the ground in such great numbers.

THE NINTH PLAGUE   **EXODUS 10:21-29**

Darkness covered the entire land for three days.

THE TENTH PLAGUE   **EXODUS 12: 1-42**

The tenth plague was the slaying of the first-born. This was preceded by the Passover.

LEVITICUS

This book contains instructions for the Levites – the clergy for whom the book is named and to others concerning holiness. Many laws relate to animal sacrifices, but every law is related in one way or another to the need for personal holiness and being in relationship with God. Leviticus is one of the most important books of the Old Testament. Without an understanding of the principles of atonement and holiness found in Leviticus, much of the New Testament has no foundation on which to rest.

Two basic themes are developed around the focal point of atonement. The first major emphasis is concerned with removing the defilement that separates man from God. The second major concern involves the means by which the disrupted fellowship between man and God can be restored.

AUTHOR: Moses

APPROXIMATE DATE: 1445 – 1405 B.C.

THEME: Atonement and Holiness

MAJOR CONTENTS
1. The sacrificial system (1-7)
2. Priestly ordination (8-10)
3. Clean and unclean (11-15)
4. The Day of Atonement (16)
5. A Holiness manifesto (17-27)

SCRIPTURE MEMORIZATION
Lev 11:45: For I am the Lord that _____ you up out of the land of Egypt, to be your God: ye shall therefore be _____, for I am _____.

Lev 13:1-3: Who examined those who were sick of Leprosy? _____

Lev 13:45-46: What happened to those who were determined to be unclean from leprosy?

_____

_____

_____

_____

THE ARK OF THE COVENANT

The Ark of the Covenant was one of the most holy pieces of furniture ever made.
It consisted of a rectangular chest made of shittim wood and covered over with gold. God had commanded Moses to make the Ark of the Covenant and inside it Moses placed the two tables of the ten commandment laws. Later on, Aaron's rod was placed in it. The mercy seat was a kind of lid which closed the chest from above. It was made of pure gold and was held in place by a golden ridge or crown. Beaten out of this mercy seat were two cherubim angels, which with their wings overshadowed the mercy seat.

✝ Ark of the Covenant entirely covered with gold – Exodus 25:11; Exodus 37:2

✝ Furnished with rings and staves – Exodus 25:12-15; Exodus 37:3-5

✝ Tables of testimony placed in it– Exodus 25:16-21; 1 Kings 8:9,21; 2 Chronicles 5:10; Hebrews 9:4

✝ Mercy seat laid upon it – Exodus 25:21; Exodus 26:34

✝ Ark was placed in the Holy of Holies – Exodus 26:33; Exodus 40:21; Hebrews 9:3-4

✝ Aaron's rod laid up before– Hebrews 9:4; Exodus 16:33-34; Numbers 17:10

✝ The pot of manna in it – Exodus 16:32-36

✝ A copy of the law "Pentateuch" lay inside of it –Deuteronomy 31:25-26

✝ Anointed with sacred oil – Exodus 30:26

✝ Ark was covered with the veil by the priests before removal – Numbers 4:5-6

✝ Ark was holy – 2 Chronicles 35:3

✝ Ark sanctified its resting place – 2 Chronicles 8:11

✝ Ark was carried by the priests– Deuteronomy 10:8; Joshua 3:14; 2 Samuel 15:24; 1 Chronicles 15:2

MIRACLES CONNECTED WITH THE ARK

✝ Jordan River divided – Joshua Chapters 3 and 4

✝ Fall of the walls of Jericho – Joshua 6:6-20

✝ Punishment falling on Eli's Sons –1 Samuel 4:5-18

✝ Fall of Dagon – 1 Samuel 5:1-4

✝ Philistines plagued with tumors – 1 Samuel 5:6-12

✝ Manner of its restoration – 1 Samuel 6:1-18

✝ Death of the men at Beth Shemesh for looking inside the ark. – 1 Samuel 6:19-21

NUMBERS

This book is called Numbers from the several numberings of the people contained in it. It extends from the giving of the law at Sinai, till their arrival in the plains of Jordan. An account is given of their murmuring and unbelief, for which they were sentenced to wander in the wilderness for forty years.

APPROXIMATE DATE: 1445-1405 B.C.

AUTHOR: Moses

THEME: Consequences; Wilderness Wanderings

MAJOR CONTENTS
1. Preparations for departure from Sinai (1:1 – 10:10)
2. Traveling from Sinai to Kadesh (10:11 – 20:21)
3. The bronze snake (21:4-9)
4. Traveling from Kadesh to Moab   (20:22 – 36:13)
5. Man was spoken to by a donkey (22:28-30)

SCRIPTURE MEMORIZATION
Num 14:6-7: What two Canaan spies came back with good reports?

_____ and _____

In Exo 17:6: God told Moses to hit the rock and he obeyed God. In Num 20:7-12: God told Moses to _____to the rock but instead Moses 'hit' the rock twice. Why do you think Moses was disobedient and how did God punish Moses for disobeying Him?

_____

_____

_____

In Num 21: How do the Israelites compare to us today and how does the Bronze Snake represent that we should look to our Redeemer and live!

_____

_____

Num 23:19: God is not a _____, that he should _____; neither the son of man, that he should _____: hath he said, and shall he not do it? or hath he _____, and shall he not make it good?

35

DEUTERONOMY

The book of Deuteronomy is an account of events spoken by Moses to the Israelites just before they were to enter the promised land. This book repeats much of the history and laws contained in the three foregoing books. Moses delivered it to Israel a little before his death. Moses, now an older man, summarizes the history of the Jewish nation. Joshua is chosen as Moses' successor to lead the people into the "promised land" they have been looking forward to settling in for forty years. This book is often referred to as "everyman's torah."

AUTHOR: Moses

APPROXIMATE DATE: 15th Century B.C.

THEME: Preparation for the Promised Land

MAJOR CONTENTS
1. Remember the past (1:12 - 4:40)
2. One who had a bed 13½ feet long and 6 feet wide (3:11)
3. The Ten Commandments (5:7-21)
4. Be careful in the future (4:41 - 11:32)
5. The Laws of Deuteronomy (12-26)
6. The women who had to shave their heads (21:11-13)
7. Blessings and curses (27:1 - 31:6)
8. Moses' farewell and death (31:7 - 34:12)

SCRIPTURE MEMORIZATION

Deu 6:5: And thou shalt _____ the Lord thy God with all thine _____, and with all thy _____, and with all thy _____.

Deu 8:1: All the _____ which I command thee this day shall ye _____ to do, that ye may live, and _____, and go in and _____ the land which the Lord sware unto your fathers.

Deu 9:11: How long was Moses up on the mountain when God gave him the Ten Commandments? _____

Deu 34:5-7: How old was Moses when he died, and where was he buried? _____

_____

Deu 34:9: Who succeeded Moses as leader of the Israelites? _____

THE LAW (TORAH) - 05 BOOKS

APPLIED LEARNING PAGE

GENESIS	**AUTHOR: MOSES**
EXODUS	**AUTHOR: MOSES**
LEVITICUS	**AUTHOR: MOSES**
NUMBERS	**AUTHOR: MOSES**
DEUTERONOMY	**AUTHOR: MOSES**

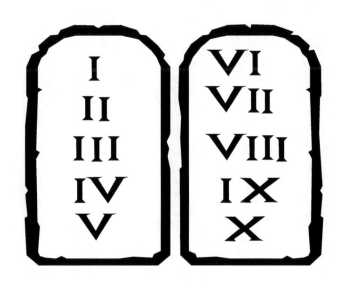

APPLICATION

Write a sentence or song using the first letters of each book to help you memorize the five books of the law. Do not move to the next section until you have learned the 05 books of the law. Members of Christian Deliverance Ministry School of Education came up with:

EXAMPLE:	**G**enesis	**E**xodus	**L**eviticus	**N**umbers	**D**euteronomy
	God	**E**xpects	**L**ove	**N**ight &	**D**ay
	God's	**E**ternal	**L**ove	**N**ever	**D**ies

FUN LEARNING

Apply some of the fun learning techniques from the learning techniques page and repeat as needed.

APPLIED LEARNING PAGE

How many books are in the Bible? _____

How many books are in the OT? _____

How many books are in the NT? _____

What language was the OT originally written in? _____

What language was the NT originally written in? _____

How many years did it take to write the Bible? _____

How many authors wrote the Bible? _____

What year was the King James Version written? _____

What year was the first Bible printed? _____

What does BC stand for? _____

What does AD stand for? _____

What language is AD in? _____

What does BCE stand for? _____

What does CE stand for? _____

Who wrote the first 5 books of the Bible? _____

Write down the first 5 books of the Bible _____

_____

_____

_____

_____

What are TWO other names for the books of "LAW"? _____

_____

APPLIED LEARNING PAGE

DETAIL THE DAYS OF CREATION

DAY ONE   _____

DAY TWO   _____

DAY THREE   _____

DAY FOUR   _____

DAY FIVE   _____

DAY SIX   _____

DAY SEVEN   _____

GOD CREATED MAN ON THE SIXTH DAY

MAN'S CREATION DIFFERS FROM THAT OF THE ANIMALS IN THAT HE IS MADE
IN THE IMAGE AND LIKENESS OF GOD.

IN YOUR OWN WORDS DESCRIBE HOW MAN HAS DISAPPOINTED GOD.

_____

_____

_____

_____

_____

_____

_____

APPLIED LEARNING PAGE

What book includes the story of the Red Sea? _____

What book includes the story of Noah's Ark? _____

List the 10 Plagues with Pharaoh. What book includes the 10 Plaques? _____

1._____	2._____
3._____	4._____
5._____	6._____
7._____	8._____
9._____	10._____

Why did God change the languages at the Tower of Babel? *(Read Genesis 11)*

_____

_____

_____

What are the 3 steps to Bible Study after you pray? *(Page 12)*

_____

_____

_____

Should you use a commentary (Before) or (After) you read the scripture? Why? *(Page 11)*

_____

HOW MANY YEARS ARE BETWEEN?

2000 B.C.   **-0-**   2000 A.D.

← ———————————————————————————————— →

B.C.   **A.D.**

2000 B.C. THROUGH 2000 A.D   _____

1900 B.C. THROUGH 1700 B.C   _____

1000 A.D. THROUGH 1500 A.D   _____

WHO IS MOSES?

Moses is one of the best-known people of the Bible. He played a key role in the Exodus, during which he received the Ten Commandments from God. He directed the construction of the tabernacle and the Ark of the Covenant. He is also the author of the Pentateuch.

✝ Moses was a Levite (Exodus 2:1), son of Amram and Jochebed (Exodus 6:20), brother of Aaron and Miriam (1 Chronicles 6:3). Moses had a speech impediment (Exodus 4:10) and God used his brother Aaron as a mouthpiece for Moses (Exodus 4:14-16)

✝ Moses was born in Egypt (Exodus 2:1-2). To escape the Egyptian king's order to kill all male Hebrew infants (Exodus 1:15-16), Moses' mother hid him for 3 months and after she could no longer hide him she put him in a basket, and set the basket floating in the Nile River (Exodus 2:3-4).

✝ The basket was found by Pharaoh's sister, who ended up adopted Moses. She named him Moses, meaning, "I drew him out of the water." (Exodus 2:5-10) Moses grew up in the palace of Pharaoh where he was educated in all the wisdom of the Egyptians.

✝ After he had grown up, Moses killed an Egyptian who had been abusing a Hebrew (Exodus 2:11-12). When Pharaoh learned of the killing, he tried to kill Moses, but Moses fled for his life into the desert of Sinai (Exodus 2:14-15). There he met Jethro, a priest of Midian. Moses married one of Jethro's daughters named Zipporah (Exodus 2:15-22).

✝ When his time of training was completed, God appeared to Moses in the burning bush and gave him his mission - the Exodus (Exodus 3:1-22). Moses was 80 years old at the time of the Exodus. He had spent 40 years in the palace of Pharaoh (learning how to govern), and 40 years in the Sinai (learning how to live in the Sinai wilderness) - all in preparation for the next 40 years, which would be spent on the wilderness journey.

✝ Moses Sister, Miriam, and Brother, Aaron, began to talk against Moses because of his Cushite wife. They also began to frown on Moses' prophetic role. God judged Miriam with leprosy. After Moses prayed to the Lord to heal her, Miriam's health was restored following a seven day confinement outside the camp (Numbers 11:35; Numbers 12:1-15).

TEN COMMANDMENTS QUIZ
EXODUS 20:1-17 OR DEUTERONOMY 5

1. "Thou shalt have no other gods before me" is which commandment?

- ☐ Third
- ☐ First
- ☐ Tenth
- ☐ Fifth

2. "Thou shalt not commit adultery" is which commandment?

- ☐ Seventh
- ☐ Tenth
- ☐ Fourth
- ☐ Ninth

3. "Thou shalt not steal" is which commandment?

- ☐ Fourth
- ☐ Seventh
- ☐ Eighth
- ☐ Second

4. "Thou shalt not make unto thee any graven images" is which commandment?

- ☐ Ninth
- ☐ Fourth
- ☐ Tenth
- ☐ Second

5. We are told not to covet the things of our neighbors in which commandment?

- ☐ Second
- ☐ Tenth
- ☐ Ninth
- ☐ Seventh

TEN COMMANDMENTS QUIZ
EXODUS 20:1-17 OR DEUTERONOMY 5

6. "Thou shalt not bear false witness against thy neighbour" is which commandment?

- ☐ Ninth
- ☐ Third
- ☐ Fifth
- ☐ Sixth

7. "Thou shalt not take the name of the Lord thy God in vain" is which commandment?

- ☐ First
- ☐ Second
- ☐ Third
- ☐ Fourth

8. "Honor thy father and thy mother" is which commandment?

- ☐ Fourth
- ☐ Fifth
- ☐ Seventh
- ☐ Eighth

9. "Thou shalt not kill" is which commandment?

- ☐ First
- ☐ Fourth
- ☐ Second
- ☐ Sixth

10. "Remember the Sabbath day, to keep it holy" is which commandment?

- ☐ Fourth
- ☐ Fifth
- ☐ Third
- ☐ Second

THE LAW (TORAH) - 05 BOOKS
COURSEWORK

HOMEWORK ASSIGNMENTS

QUESTIONS I HAVE FOR A BIBLE TEACHER

SECTION SPECIAL NOTES

THE HISTORY - 12 BOOKS

JOSHUA

JUDGES

RUTH

1 SAMUEL

2 SAMUEL

1 KINGS

2 KINGS

1 CHRONICLES

2 CHRONICLES

EZRA

NEHEMIAH

ESTHER

JOSHUA

JOSHUA name, originally "Hoshea" (Numbers 13:8), meaning "salvation," Moses changed Hoshea to "Joshua" meaning "Yahweh is salvation" (Numbers 13:16). Joshua is a book of war and conquest, including the famous attack on the city of Jericho. Joshua was one of the twelve men sent by Moses to explore the land (Numbers 13:16-17), but only Joshua and Caleb gave an encouraging report. After the death of Moses, Joshua carried out the work started by Moses. God promised Joshua, as I was with Moses, so will I be with you; I will never leave you nor forsake you. "Be strong and courageous, because you will lead these people to inherit the land I swore to their forefathers to give them." (Joshua 1:1-6)

AUTHOR: Joshua

APPROXIMATE DATE: 14th Century B.C.

THEME: The theme of Joshua is the Lord's gift of the land to Israel as a demonstration of His faithfulness, power, and justice

MAJOR CONTENTS
1. Crossing the Jordan (1:1 - 5:12)
2. The conquest of Jericho (5:13 - 6:27)
3. The conquest of Ai (7-8)
4. Campaigns in central, southern, and northern Canaan (9-12)
5. Sun stood still for a whole day (10:13)
6. Settlement of the tribes in Canaan (13-19)
7. The Levitical cities and cities of refuge (20-21)
8. The Trans-Jordan crisis (22)
9. Joshua's farewell challenge and death (23-24)

JOSHUA FOUGHT THE BATTLE OF JERICHO SONG CHORUS:
Joshua fought the battle of Jericho Jericho Jericho;
Joshua fought the battle of Jericho; And the walls came tumbling down.

SCRIPTURE MEMORIZATION
Josh 6:12-16: There were _____ priests with Joshua when he marched

around Jericho _____ times. On the last day how many times

did they march around Jericho within that one day? _____

Josh 24:15: And if it seem _____ unto you to _____ the Lord,

_____ you this day whom ye will serve; whether the gods which your

fathers served that were on the other side of the flood, or the gods of the Amorites, in whose

land ye dwell: but as for me and my house, we will _____ the Lord.

JUDGES

The book of Judges is the history of Israel during the government of the Judges, who were occasional deliverers, raised up by God to rescue Israel from their oppressors, to reform the state of religion, and to administer justice to the people. One thing that stands out is that the conquest was incomplete and fighting remained. However, the fighting in Judges is forced upon Israel (defensive, rather than offensive – Ephesians 6:10-19).

AUTHOR: Unknown. Some suggest **Samuel**

APPROXIMATE DATE: 11th Century B.C.

THEME: Disobedience and God's Faithfulness

MAJOR CONTENTS
1. Status of the conquest after Joshua (1:1 - 2:10)
2. Summary of the "Judges" cycle (2:11 - 3:4)
3. The Judges of Israel (3:5 - 16:31)
4. Gideon defeats the Midianites (7-1-25)
5. Samson and Delilah (16-1-31)
6. Conditions and crisis during the period of the Judges (17-21)
7. An army with 700 left handed men (20:16)

SCRIPTURE MEMORIZATION

Judges 7:1-7: How many men did Gideon originally have with him? _____.

How many men were fearful and afraid? _____. How many

men did Gideon take to fight the Midianites? _____.

Judges 15:15: What did Samson use to fight off a thousand men?

_____

Judges 16:18: What woman betrayed Samson? _____

Judges 17:6: In those days there was no _____ in _____, but

every man did that which was _____ in his own _____.

FIFTEEN JUDGES OF ISRAEL

When Joshua died, Israel was left without a leader. So the Lord rose up "Judges" who led the people of Israel, turning them from their worship of "Baal" and idol worship. The Judges offered guidance to the people of Israel.

OTHNIEL	Judges 3:7-11	Othniel was the first Judge. He delivered Israel from the Mesopotamians.
EHUD	Judges 3:12-30	Ehud was left handed and killed the fat man Eglon. By being left handed, he could conceal his sword on his right thigh.
SHAMGAR	Judges 3:31	Shamgar was praised for killing 600 Philistines with an ox goad.
DEBORAH	Judges 4:1 - 5:31	Only Female "Judge" said to be a "mother of Israel." Deborah was also a Prophetess.
GIDEON	Judges 6:1 - 8:35	Gideon led 300 Israelites to defeat the entire army of 135,000 Midianites.
ABIMELECH	Judges 9:1-57	Conspired to assassinate all 70 of his brothers and establish himself as king. His youngest brother, Jotham, hid himself and escaped the slaughter.
TOLA	Judges 10:1-2	Tola was the first of the minor Judges. Judged for 23 years.
JAIR	Judges 10:3-5	Judged for 22 years. Followed Tola as the second so-called minor Judges of Israel.
JEPHTHAH	Judges 10:6 - 12:7	Jephthah was a harlot's son (Judges 11:1) who defeated the Amorites.
IBZAN	Judges 12:8-10	Found husbands for all 30 of his daughters and also brought in wives for all 30 of his sons. Assumed to be wealthy.
ELON	Judges 12:11-12	One of the minor Judges who judged Israel for 10 years.
ABDON	Judges 12:13-15	Abdon had 40 sons. Judged Israel for 8 years.
SAMSON	Judges 13:1 - 16:31	Delivered Israel from the Philistines. Known for his great strength.
ELI	I Samuel 1:1 - 4:22	Suffered the downfall of his house and violent deaths of his two evil sons.
SAMUEL	I Samuel 1:1 - 25:1	Samuel, who was dedicated to the service of the Lord before his birth, became a prophet and Judge. He anointed the first two kings of Israel, Saul and David. Last of the Judges.

RUTH

The book is simply titled, with the name of the main character - a Moabite woman named Ruth. Ruth is the story of a beautiful young widow who comes to Israel from a foreign land. Ruth shows us that there was faith and godliness (Jews & Moabites) during a time of apostasy. This book is an excellent example of faith, piety, patience, humility, industry, and loving-kindness, in the common events of life. The book of Ruth is the story of how Ruth became an ancestor of Jesus Christ. This is one of two books in the Bible after a woman's name (Ruth and Esther).

AUTHOR: Unknown: Many name Samuel as author; others suggest Hezekiah, Ezra, or even David as the writers.

APPROXIMATE DATE: 1010-970 B.C.

THEME: Faithfulness and Redemption Love

MAJOR CONTENTS
1. Naomi and Ruth returns to Judah (1)
2. Ruth gleans in Boaz' field (2)
3. Boaz promises to redeem Ruth (3)
4. The marriage of Ruth (4)

SCRIPTURE MEMORIZATION

Ruth 1:16: And _____ said, Entreat me not to leave thee, or to return from following after thee: for whither thou _____, I will go; and where thou lodgest, I will lodge: thy _____ shall be my people, and thy _____ my _____.

Ruth 2:10-23: Why did Boaz find favor with Ruth? _____

_____

Ruth 4:9-10: Whom did Ruth marry? _____

Ruth 4:14-17: What was Ruth's relationship to King David? _____

1 & 2 SAMUEL

The first two divisions bear the name of Samuel - prophet, priest, and anointer of kings. The scrolls of long ago could only hold so much handwritten information before they became too large to handle. The book of Samuel was one of these books, so it was divided into two parts: First and Second Samuel. The two books of Samuel present a continuous account of the history of Israel from the end of the period of the Judges to David's latter years. In this book we have an account of Eli, and the wickedness of his sons; also of Samuel, his character and actions. Then of the advancement of Saul to be the first king of Israel, and his ill behavior, until his death made way for David's progression to the throne. Many things in this book encourage the faith, hope, and patience of the suffering believer.

AUTHOR: Unknown. Many suggest Samuel

APPROXIMATE DATE: Probably between 1050 and 931 B.C.

1 SAMUEL THEME: The book describes the growing desire for a king, the differing opinions that accompanied that desire, and the roles that various individuals played in the beginning and continuing days of Hebrew kingship.

2 SAMUEL THEME: The Reign of David: Although the books of Samuel were originally one volume in the Hebrew text, the English translation, which is patterned after the Greek, divides the book into two parts. Second Samuel is concerned solely with the character of David.

MAJOR CONTENTS
1. Samuel as Judge (1 Samuel 1-7)
2. Samuel and King Saul (1 Samuel 8-15)
3. David kills Goliath (1 Samuel 17:1-51)
4. King Saul and David (1 Samuel 16 – 2 Samuel 1)
5. David as King of Judah and Israel (2 Samuel 2-8)
6. Events at David's court (2 Samuel 9-20)
7. David and Bathsheba (2 Samuel 11)
8. Man who had 12 fingers and 12 toes (2 Samuel 21:20)
9. David's Latter reign (2 Samuel 21-24)

SCRIPTURE MEMORIZATION

1 Sam 1:20: What was the name of the baby boy that God gave Hannah? _____

1 Sam 3:1: Who took care of Samuel in the temple? _____

1 Sam 15:22-23: Behold, to _____ is better than _____,
and to _____ than the fat of rams. For rebellion is as the sin of _____,
and stubbornness is as iniquity and _____. Because thou hast
_____ the word of the Lord, he hath also rejected thee from being king.

1 Sam 17:48-51: Who was killed with a stone and sword? _____

2 Sam 4:4: What's the name of the child who was dropped by his nurse when he was five
years old and became crippled for life? _____

2 Sam 7:22: Wherefore thou art _____, O Lord God: for there is none like thee,
neither is there any _____ beside thee, according to all that we have _____
with our ears.

2 Sam 11:2-27: Who was the wife of Uriah? _____. Who had an affair with
Uriah's wife? _____. What happened to Uriah? _____;
This affair _____ God. 2 Sam 12:18: What happen to the first baby they
had? _____; 2 Sam 12:24: What was the name of the
second baby they had? _____.

What are some of the things you learn from this adulterous relationship? _____

_____

_____

2 Sam 13: Problems continued in David's family. Read the story of Absalom, Amnon and
Tamar. List all the things you learn from this story.

_____

_____

_____

1 & 2 KINGS

The history of Israel's kings continues, including the wisest and richest (Solomon) and the most evil (Ahab—with help from his queen, Jezebel). Even God's prophets and the idol-worshiping priests of Baal join in the conflict. First and Second Kings was originally one book.

AUTHOR: Unknown. Possibly more than one author

APPROXIMATE DATE: Shortly after 560 B.C.

THEME: Israel's Rejection of the Covenant

MAJOR CONTENTS
1. The reign of Solomon (1 Kings 1-11)
2. Elijah-the prophets of Baal (1 Kings 18)
3. God speaks to Elijah (1 Kings 19)
4. Elisha and healing of Naaman (2 Kings 5)
5. The Southern Kingdom to the Exile (2 Kings 18-25)

SCRIPTURE MEMORIZATION

1 Ki 3:24-25: What was Solomon's solution to the two women both claiming that a particular baby was theirs? How did this show great wisdom? _____

_____

1 Ki 6:38: How many years did it take Solomon to complete the original temple in Jerusalem?

_____

1 Ki 8:11: So that the priests could not stand to _____because of the cloud: for the _____of the Lord had filled the house of the Lord.

1 Ki 11:3: How many wives did King Solomon have? _____

1 Ki 19:16: Whom did Elijah anoint to follow him? _____

2 Ki 2:19-21: What did Elisha throw into the dirty waters of Jericho? _____

2 Ki 5:10: Which river was Naaman to wash in seven times? _____

2 Ki 13:21: A man came back to life when his body touched the bones of which prophet?

_____

2 Ki 20:1: In those days was _____ sick unto death. And the prophet _____the son of Amoz came to him, and said unto him, thus saith the Lord, Set thine _____ in order; for thou shalt _____, and not_____.

1 & 2 CHRONICLES

First Chronicles is sort of a combination of Numbers and Kings. Chronicles is a history of the Hebrew people. The first book traces the rise of the Jewish people from Adam, and afterward gives an account of the reign of David. In the second book the narrative is continued, and relates the progress and end of the kingdom of Judah; also it notices the return of the Jews from Babylon's captivity. The purpose of the Chronicler was to comprehend the rationale of Israel's history in relation to the Mosaic Law. The books of 1 and 2 Chronicles were originally one book.

AUTHOR: Unknown. Some suggest Ezra

APPROXIMATE DATE: Fifth Century B.C.

THEME: Chronicles emphasizes the faithfulness of God to His people, the power of the Word of God, and the central role of worship in the lives of God's people. Second Chronicles recounts the downfall of the Davidic dynasty from Solomon to the Exile. The Chronicles were written to the returned remnants who were rebuilding Jerusalem following their seventy-year Babylonian captivity. The history of the southern kingdom (Judah) is presented in such a way as to help restore its religious and national heritage by showing its unbroken connection with the patriarchal beginnings. The primary historical theme centers about the priestly worship of Judah, from the time of Saul until the return of the Jewish nation to the land following the decree of Cyrus.

MAJOR CONTENTS
1. Genealogical material (1 Chronicles 1-9)
2. The rule of David (1 Chronicles 10-29)
3. The rule of Solomon (2 Chronicles 1-9)
4. The later history of Judah (2 Chronicles 10-36)
5. Father who had eighty-eight children (2 Chronicles 11:21)

1 & 2 CHRONICLES

SCRIPTURE MEMORIZATION

1 Chr 2:1-2: What were the names of Jacob's 12 sons from whom the 12 tribes of Israel originated? (Review pages 25-29) _____

_____

1 Chr 15:2: Who were the only people permitted to carry the Ark of the Covenant?

_____

1 Chr 16:22: Saying, touch not mine _____, and do my _____ no harm.

1 Chr 16:29: Give unto the Lord the _____ due unto his name: bring an _____, and come before him: worship the Lord in the beauty of _____.

1 Chr 29:26-27: How long did David reign over Israel? _____

2 Chr 7:14: If my people, which are called by my name, shall _____ themselves, and _____, and _____ my face, and _____ from their wicked ways; then will I _____from heaven, and will forgive their sin, and will_____ their land.

2 Chr 11:21: How many children did Rehoboam have? _____

2 Chr 16:12: And Asa in the thirty and ninth year of his reign was diseased in his _____, until his disease was exceeding great: yet in his disease he sought not to the Lord, but to the _____*(What do you learn from this story?)* _____

_____

_____

2 Chr 26:20: What sickness did God strike Uzziah with? _____

EZRA

After the fall of the Babylonian Empire, the Persian king allowed some Jewish captives to return to their homeland with Ezra. This book focuses on their return and the rebuilding of their city, temple, and lives. Surrounded by enemies, it was not easy. From its contents we especially learn, that every good work will meet with opposition from enemies, but that God will make His cause prevail over the blockades of the adversary.

AUTHOR: Unknown. Some suggest Ezra or Nehemiah.

APPROXIMATE DATE: 450 B.C.

THEME: The Restoration of the People of God

MAJOR CONTENTS
1. Cyrah permits Jews to return to Judah under Zerubbabel (1)
2. A genealogical register of those returning to Judah (2)
3. Altar set up and temple foundations laid (3)
4. Enemies oppose the building of the temple and Artaxerxes orders it to stop (4)
5. The temple work to resume (5-6)
6. The scribe, Ezra, returns to Judah (7-8)
7. Ezra deals with the mixed marriage problem (9-10)

SCRIPTURE MEMORIZATION
Select two scriptures from this book to memorize and recite.

NEHEMIAH

Nehemiah, sort of a "religious storm trooper," decides Israel has taken enough abuse from their enemies and organizes the rebuilding of a fortified wall surrounding Jerusalem.

AUTHOR: Probably Nehemiah

APPROXIMATE DATE: 430-420 B.C.

THEME: God's Provision for His People. The book of Nehemiah was written to document the provisions, both physical and spiritual, that God made for the defense of His people.

MAJOR CONTENTS
1. Nehemiah returns to Judah to rebuild Jerusalem's walls (1-6)
2. Registry of citizens (7)
3. Renewal of the covenant (8-10)
4. Jerusalem re-populated, Temple worship reformed (11-12)
5. Nehemiah returns from Persia and deals with problems (13)

SCRIPTURE MEMORIZATION

Nehemiah 4:6: So built we the _____; and all the wall was joined together

unto the half thereof: for the people had a _____ to work.

ESTHER

The book of Esther displays the infinite wisdom, continuing providence, and overwhelming power of God in the preservation of His people. Even the most insignificant events and ordinary happenings of the world, with its rulers and subjects, are appointed and directed by God to effect His purposes. This book was named after Esther and is the only other Bible book besides, Ruth, named after a woman.

DID YOU KNOW?
The name of "God" appears in every book of the Bible except Esther and Song of Solomon.

AUTHOR: Unknown

APPROXIMATE DATE: Fifth Century B.C.

THEME: God's Providence for Israel

MAJOR CONTENTS
1. Hadassah (Esther) rises to prominence (1-2)
2. Haman's plot to kill Mordecai's people, the Jews (3)
3. Esther Intercedes for her people (4-7)
4. Mordecai promoted and Jews warned of Haman's plot (8)
5. The Jews defend themselves and feast of Purim instituted (9-10)

SCRIPTURE MEMORIZATION

Esther 2:7:   Who adopted Esther? _____

Esther 4:16a: And if I _____ I perish.

Esther 4 thru 7:   How did Esther intercede for her people? _____

_____

THE HISTORY - 12 BOOKS
COURSEWORK

HOMEWORK ASSIGNMENTS

| |
| |
| |
| |
| |
| |
| |

QUESTIONS I HAVE FOR A BIBLE TEACHER

| |
| |
| |
| |
| |
| |
| |

SECTION SPECIAL NOTES

| |
| |
| |
| |
| |
| |

KINGS OF ISRAEL

KING SAUL

After about 350 years of being ruled by Judges (see page 48), the people of Israel demanded to have a King. Israel's government until the time of Saul was a theocracy- meaning a government with God as the King. Rather than allowing God to be their King, the Israelites wanted to have a King like the neighboring countries. God warned them that if they chose a King to rule over them that the King would eventually treat them with hardship. Yet, they insisted on a King to be like the other nations. The choice fell upon Saul, a Benjaminite renowned for his bravery and great height. Saul was tall and sturdy, pious, and intelligent. He lived and worked with his father on their farm. When the Bible introduces us to Saul, he is unsuccessfully searching for his father's donkeys. He returns being made a King privately anointed by Samuel (1 Samuel 10:1). Little did Saul realize that his obedience in going to search for his father's donkeys would end the way it did. Later in life, Saul made choices contrary to the will of God and as a result the spirit of God left Saul (1 Samuel 16:14). His kingdom was taken from him and he was replaced by his son-in-law, David (1 Samuel 13). As Israel trembles by the sight of the giant Goliath, David's bravery saves the day. After the victory, the women of Israel sang that Saul has slain his thousands; and David, his tens of thousands. Saul became jealous of David and tried killing him several times. As Saul falls, David rises. During a battle with the Philistines, Saul's three sons were killed and he himself fell upon his own sword. The Philistines hung Saul's body and the bodies of his sons.

KING DAVID

David was the second King of Israel. He was the youngest son of Jesse of Bethlehem and descendant of Ruth. David became King of Israel after the death of the rebellious Saul, and thus began the golden age of Israel. The Prophet Samuel anointed David to be King after Saul died. David made Jerusalem the political and religious center of his kingdom, building a palace for himself on its highest hill (city of David), and placing the Ark of the Covenant there under a tent. Although David laid an extensive organizational and engineering foundation for building the Temple (1 Chronicles 22), God did not grant him the privilege of actually building the Temple. The Bible says that it was because David had shed much blood on the earth (1 Chronicles 22:8). David was succeeded by Solomon, his son with Bathsheba. Although David sinned in adultery and murder he repented and is stated to be a man after God's own heart. He never worshipped the pagan gods his son, Solomon, eventually worshipped and even in his wrongdoing, he knew how to repent and talk to the living God.

KING SOLOMON

King David's son, Solomon, inherited a prosperous kingdom. Building on David's achievements, he established an efficient centralized government. He carried out his father's plan to erect a Temple for the Lord, worthy to house the Ark of the Covenant. The Bible provides a vivid description of the Temple's dedication in 1 Kings 6-8. The Temple's gold-inlaid doors swung open as the Ark was brought into the large vestibule and finally into its resting place inside the Holy of Holies. Solomon led the procession of the Elders and heads of Israel's tribes behind the Ark. Solomon's Temple made Jerusalem not just another capital, but Israel's religious center. Solomon's 40 year reign and building of the Temple became a high point in Bible History. His fame was widespread and he received visitors from all parts of the world. The Queen of Sheba came to discover for herself, whether all she had heard about Solomon and his kingdom were really true. She had to confess that the half had not been told! Solomon's wisdom and wealth made him the greatest king who ever lived. The first and most famous incident of his wisdom was when two women came to his court with a baby whom both women claimed as their own. Solomon threatened to split the baby in half. One woman was prepared to accept the decision, but the other begged the King to give the live baby to the other woman. Solomon then knew the second woman was the mother. The Bible gives us the reasons for the king's downfall. He loved many strange women and he allowed them to continue their own forms of worship, defiling the Holy City with their foreign rituals and gods. Solomon not only tolerated this paganism but also indulged in it himself. He even used his skills of building the temple to build places of worship for the pagan gods (1 Kings 11:7). Solomon had 700 wives and 300 concubines (1 Kings 11:3). After King Solomon died the Kingdom of Israel was divided by political and religious differences into two kingdoms. Unwilling to be ruled by Solomon's son, Rehoboam, ten tribes split off and joined together as the northern kingdom, which retained the title of Israel. The southern kingdom (Benjamin and Judah) joined together and became known as the Tribe of Judah, and Jerusalem was the capital city. Rehoboam became King of the Southern Kingdom and Jeroboam became king over the Northern Kingdom. These two kingdoms were constantly at strife with each other. God warned Israel and Judah over and over again through the prophets. The people forsook God, worshipped idols, did injustice, and loved evil. But God was kind enough to forewarn them of coming judgments. Israel's history demonstrates that when they broke the laws God gave them, they experienced exactly the results God predicted would happen if they were unfaithful. Solomon shone in Israel's memory as a man wiser than all men. He is the writer of Proverbs, Ecclesiastes and Song of Solomon.

✝ Saul reigned 40 years, Acts 13:21.

✝ David reigned 40 years over all Israel, 2 Samuel 5:3-4.

✝ Solomon reigned 40 years, 1 Kings 11:42 and 2 Chronicles 9:30.

SOLOMON'S TEMPLE

After seven long years of construction all of Israel came to witness Solomon's Temple. The Temple was a most spectacular and expensive construction project. Solomon covered the inside of the Temple with pure gold. He also covered the floors of both the inner and outer rooms of the Temple with gold (1 Kings 6:20-30). Solomon constructed the temple on Mt. Moriah, north of the ancient City of David. The temple was built according to plans that David received from the Lord and passed on to Solomon (1 Chronicles 28:11-19). The division into a sanctuary and inner sanctuary corresponds to the division of the tabernacle into the holy place and most holy place. Solomon's Temple was destroyed by Nebuchadnezzar in 587 B.C. The Temple was later rebuilt twice and then destroyed by the Romans who built a pagan temple on its site.

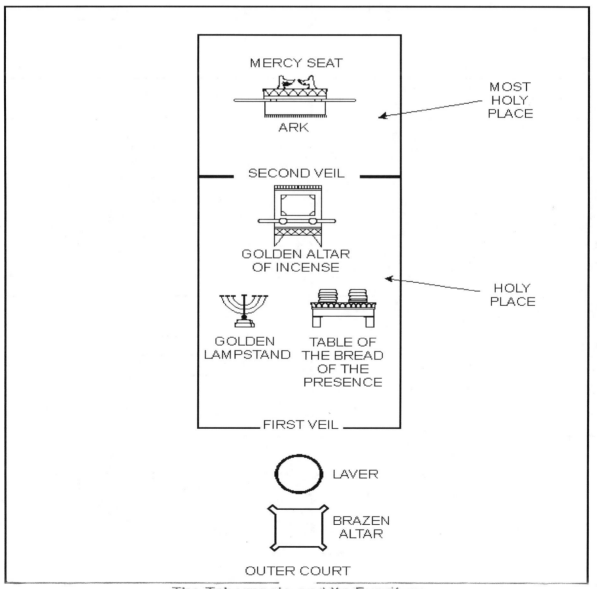

The Tabernacle and Its Furniture

RULERS OF THE UNITED KINGDOM

1. **Saul**	**1 Samuel 9:1-31:13**
2. **David**	**1 Samuel 16:1-1 Kings 2:11**
3. **Solomon**	**1 Kings 1:1-11:43**

RULERS OF THE DIVIDED KINGDOM

RULERS OF ISRAEL		RULERS OF JUDAH	
Jeroboam	1 Kgs 11:26-14:20	Rehoboam	1 Kgs 11:42-14:31
		Abijah	1 Kgs 14:31-15:8
Nadab	1 Kgs 15:25-28	Asa	1 Kgs 15:8-24
Baasha	1 Kgs 15:27-16:7		
Elah	1 Kgs 16:6-14		
Zimri	1 Kgs 16:9-20		
Omri	1 Kgs 16:15-28		
Ahab	1 Kgs 16:28-22:40	Jehoshaphat	1 Kgs 22:41-50
Ahaziah	1 Kgs 22:40 - 2 Kgs 1:18	Jehoram	2 Kgs 8:16-24
Jehoram(Joram)	2 Kgs 1:17-9:26	Ahaziah	2 Kgs 8:24-9:29
Jehu	2 Kgs 9:1-10:36	Athaliah	2 Kgs 11:1-20
Jehoahaz	2 Kgs 13:1-9	Joash	2 Kgs 11:1-12:21
Jehoash	2 Kgs 13:10-14:16	Amaziah	2 Kgs 14:1-20
Jeroboam II	2 Kgs 14:23-29	Azariah	2 Kgs 14:21; 15:1-7
Zechariah	2 Kgs 14:29-15:12		
Shallum	2 Kgs 15:10-15	Jotham	2 Kgs 15:32-38
Menahem	2 Kgs 15:14-22		
Pekahiah	2 Kgs 15:22-26		
Pekah	2 Kgs 15:25-31	Ahaz (Jehoahaz)	2 Kgs 16:1-20
Hoshea	2 Kgs 15:30-17:6		
		Hezekiah	2 Kgs 18:1-20:21
		Manasseh	2 Kgs 21:1-18
		Amon	2 Kgs 21:19-26
		Josiah	2 Kgs 21:26-23:30
		Jehoahaz II	2 Kgs 23:30-33
		Jehoiakim (Eliakim)	2 Kgs 23:34-24:5
		Jehoiachin	2 Kgs 24:6-16; 25:27-30
		Zedekiah	2 Kgs 24:17-25:7

AGES OF SOME OF THE KINGS

07 YEARS OLD   **JEHOASH**

2 Kings 11:21: Seven years old was Jehoash when he began to reign.

07 YEARS OLD   **JOASH**

2 Chronicles 24:1: Joash was seven years old when he began to reign, and he reigned forty years in Jerusalem. His mother's name also was Zibiah of Beersheba.

08 YEARS OLD   **JOSIAH**

2 Kings 22:1: Josiah was eight years old when he began to reign, and he reigned thirty and one years in Jerusalem. And his mother's name was Jedidah, the daughter of Adaiah of Boscath.

08 YEARS OLD   **JEHOIACHIN**

2 Chronicles 36:9: Jehoiachin was eight years old when he began to reign, and he reigned three months and ten days in Jerusalem: and he did that which was evil in the sight of the Lord.

12 YEARS OLD   **MANASSEH**

2 Kings 21:1: Manasseh was twelve years old when he began to reign, and reigned fifty and five years in Jerusalem. And his mother's name was Hephzibah. See also 2 Chronicles 33:1.

16 YEARS OLD   **AZARIAH**

2 Kings 15:1-2: In the twenty and seventh year of Jeroboam king of Israel began Azariah son of Amaziah king of Judah to reign. Sixteen years old was he when he began to reign, and he reigned two and fifty years in Jerusalem. And his mother's name was Jecholiah of Jerusalem.

16 YEARS OLD   **UZZIAH**

2 Chronicles 26:3: Sixteen years old was Uzziah when he began to reign, and he reigned fifty and two years in Jerusalem. His mother's name also was Jecoliah of Jerusalem.

18 YEARS OLD   **JEHOIACHIN**

2 Kings 24:8: Jehoiachin was eighteen years old when he began to reign, and he reigned in Jerusalem three months. And his mother's name was Nehushta, the daughter of Elnathan of Jerusalem.

AGES OF SOME OF THE KINGS

20 YEARS OLD   **AHAZ**

2 Kings 16:2: Twenty years old was Ahaz when he began to reign, and reigned sixteen years in Jerusalem, and did not that which was right in the sight of the Lord his God, like David his father.

21 YEARS OLD   **ZEDEKIAH**

2 Kings 24:18: Zedekiah was twenty and one years old when he began to reign, and he reigned eleven years in Jerusalem. And his mother's name was Hamutal, the daughter of Jeremiah of Libnah.

22 YEARS OLD   **AHAZIAH**

2 Kings 8:26: Two and twenty years old was Ahaziah when he began to reign; and he reigned one year in Jerusalem. And his mother's name was Athaliah, the daughter of Omri king of Israel.

22 YEARS OLD   **AMON**

2 Kings 21:19: Amon was twenty and two years old when he began to reign, and he reigned two years in Jerusalem. And his mother's name was Meshullemeth, the daughter of Haruz of Jotbah.

23 YEARS OLD   **JEHOAHAZ**

2 Kings 23:31: Jehoahaz was twenty and three years old when he began to reign; and he reigned three months in Jerusalem. And his mother's name was Hamutal, the daughter of Jeremiah of Libnah.

25 YEARS OLD   **AMAZIAH**

2 Kings 14:1-2: In the second year of Joash son of Jehoahaz king of Israel reigned Amaziah the son of Joash king of Judah. He was twenty and five years old when he began to reign, and reigned twenty and nine years in Jerusalem. And his mother's name was Jehoaddan of Jerusalem.

25 YEARS OLD   **JOTHAM**

2 Kings 15:32-33: In the second year of Pekah the son of Remaliah king of Israel began Jotham the son of Uzziah king of Judah to reign. Five and twenty years old was he when he began to reign, and he reigned sixteen years in Jerusalem. And his mother's name was Jerushah, the daughter of Zadok.

AGES OF SOME OF THE KINGS

25 YEARS OLD   **HEZEKIAH**

2 Kings 18:1-2: Now it came to pass in the third year of Hoshea son of Elah king of Israel, that Hezekiah the son of Ahaz king of Judah began to reign. Twenty and five years old was he when he began to reign; and he reigned twenty and nine years in Jerusalem. His mother's name also was Abi, the daughter of Zachariah.

25 YEARS OLD   **JEHOIAKIM**

2 Kings 23:36: Jehoiakim was twenty and five years old when he began to reign; and he reigned eleven years in Jerusalem. And his mother's name was Zebudah, the daughter of Pedaiah of Rumah.

30 YEARS OLD   **DAVID**

2 Samuel 5:4: David was thirty years old when he began to reign, and he reigned forty years.

32 YEARS OLD   **JEHORAM**

2 Kings 8:16-17: And in the fifth year of Joram the son of Ahab king of Israel, Jehoshaphat being then king of Judah, Jehoram the son of Jehoshaphat king of Judah began to reign. Thirty and two years old was he when he began to reign; and he reigned eight years in Jerusalem. Jehoram was buried in Jerusalem, but not in the graves for the kings. No one was sad when he died.

35 YEARS OLD   **JEHOSHAPHAT**

1 Kings 22:42: Jehoshaphat was thirty and five years old when he began to reign; and he reigned twenty and five years in Jerusalem. And his mother's name was Azubah the daughter of Shilhi.

40 YEARS OLD   **ISHBOSHETH**

2 Samuel 2:10: Ishbosheth Saul's son was forty years old when he began to reign over Israel, and reigned two years. But the house of Judah followed David.

41 YEARS OLD   **REHOBOAM**

1 Kings 14:21: And Rehoboam the son of Solomon reigned in Judah. Rehoboam was forty and one years old when he began to reign, and he reigned seventeen years in Jerusalem, the city which the Lord did choose out of all the tribes of Israel, to put his name there. And his mother's name was Naamah an Ammonitess.

THE KING OF KINGS

THERE WERE MANY KINGS IN THE BIBLE BUT NONE LIKE
KING JESUS
THE KING OF KINGS

I MUST BE ABOUT
MY FATHER'S BUSINESS

PSALMS 146:10: The LORD shall reign for ever, *even* thy God, O Zion, unto all generations. Praise ye the LORD.

Luke 2:42-52: And when He *(Jesus)* was _____ years old, they went up to Jerusalem after the custom of the feast. And when they had fulfilled the days, as they returned, the child Jesus tarried behind in Jerusalem; and Joseph and his mother knew not *of it*. But they, supposing Him to have been in the company, went a day's journey; and they sought Him among *their* kinsfolk and acquaintance. And when they found Him not, they turned back again to Jerusalem, seeking Him. And it came to pass, that after three days they found Him in the temple, sitting in the midst of the doctors, both hearing them, and asking them questions. And all that heard Him were astonished at his understanding and answers. And when they saw Him, they were amazed: and his mother said unto Him, Son, why hast thou thus dealt with us? Behold, thy father and I have sought thee sorrowing. And He said unto them, **how is it that ye sought me? wist ye not that I must be about my Father's business?** And they understood not the saying which He spake unto them. And He went down with them, and came to Nazareth, and was subject unto them: but His mother kept all these sayings in her heart. And Jesus increased in wisdom and stature, and in favor with God and man.

QUIZ REVIEW

IN THE RIGHT MARGIN, WRITE: (TRUE OR FALSE)

1.	There are 68 books of the Bible?	
2.	There are 39 Old Testament books of the Bible?	
3.	The King James Bible was written in 1611?	
4.	One of the Ten Commandments is Thou shall not Lie?	
5.	The Five books of the Law are Genesis, Exodus, Leviticus, Numbers, Joshua?	
6.	Exodus includes the Story of the Parting of the Red Sea?	
7.	Leviticus is the Priestly book of Laws?	
8.	The Old Testament was originally written in Greek?	
9.	A.D means After Death?	
10.	Commentaries should be read before you read the Bible chapter and verse to get a better understanding of the Bible?	
11.	On the fourth day of creation, the Lord created the sun, moon, and the stars?	

THE HISTORY - 12 BOOKS

APPLIED LEARNING PAGE

WHAT'S THE MISSING BOOK? _____

RECORD THE AUTHOR

JOSHUA   _____

JUDGES   _____

RUTH   _____

1 SAMUEL   _____

2 SAMUEL   _____

1 KINGS   _____

2 KINGS   _____

1 CHRONICLES   _____

2 CHRONICLES   _____

NEHEMIAH   _____

ESTHER   _____

WHICH BOOK DOES NOT MENTION GOD'S NAME? _____

APPLICATION
Write a sentence or song using the first letters of each book to help you memorize the history books.

FUN LEARNING
Apply some of the fun learning techniques from the learning techniques page and repeat as needed.

APPLIED LEARNING PAGE

What book comes before Exodus? _____

What book comes before Joshua? _____

What book comes before 1st Chronicles? _____

What book comes before Nehemiah? _____

Which two books are named after Women? _____

WRITE THE OT BOOKS OF LAW	WRITE THE OT HISTORY BOOKS

OLD TESTAMENT
LAW AND HISTORY BOOKS

JUDGES

1 CHRON

EZRA

EXODUS

1 SAMUEL

2 KINGS

JOSHUA

ESTHER

1 KINGS

GENESIS

DEUT

NEHEMIAH

2 CHRON

LEVITICUS

RUTH

2 SAMUEL

INSERT A NUMBER IN THE BOX TO INDICATE THE PROPER ORDER OF THE BIBLE BOOK.

NUMBERS

THE MIRACLES OF ELIJAH AND ELISHA

MIRACLES PERFORMED BY ELIJAH

1 Kings 17:1, James 5:17	Prayed that there will be no dew or rain for 3½ years
1 Kings 17:13-16, Luke 4:25	The miracle of the barrel of meal and oil
1 Kings 17:17-24	Raising of dead child
1 Kings 18:1-39	Praying down fire from heaven
1 Kings 18:1-2	Rain upon the earth following the drought
2 Kings 1:1-16	Destruction of King Ahaziah's soldiers
2 Kings 2:8	Dividing the Jordan River to walk over dry lands

MIRACLES PERFORMED BY ELISHA

2 Kings 2:14	Parting of the Jordan River
2 Kings 2:19-22	Salt in Jericho's contaminated waters causing purification
2 Kings 2:23-24	Judgment of 42 children for mocking his bald head
2 Kings 3:16-20	Valley filled with water for the Israelite army in Edom
2 Kings 4:1-7	Multiplication of oil for the widow to pay her debts
2 Kings 4:32-37	Raising of the dead Shunammite's son
2 Kings 4:38-41	Healing of the poisonous pottage stew
2 Kings 4:42-44	Multiplying barley and ears of corn for food
2 Kings 5:1-19	Healing Naaman of leprosy
2 Kings 5:26-27	Leprosy as judgment upon Gehazi
2 Kings 6:1-7	An axe head floating on the water
2 Kings 6:17	Praying for his servant eyes to be open
2 Kings 6:18	Praying for God to spite the Syrians with blindness
2 Kings 7	Delivering starving Samaria
2 Kings 13:21	Dead man revived when he touched the Bones of Elisha

POETRY - 05 BOOKS

JOB

PSALMS

PROVERBS

ECCLESIASTES

SONG OF SOLOMON

JOB

Job marvelously demonstrates the conflict of good and evil. It also shows how well-meaning friends can cause more damage than good. In Bible terms, this book is considered "wisdom literature" because of the wisdom and insight it gives to the reader. This book is so called from Job, whose prosperity, afflictions, and restoration, are recorded. He lived soon after Abraham, or perhaps before that patriarch. The instructions to be learned from the patience of Job, and from his trials, are as useful now, and as much needed as ever. We live under the same providence, we have the same chastening father, and there is the same need for correction unto righteousness. The fortitude and patience of Job, though not small, gave way in his severe troubles; but his faith was fixed upon the coming of his Redeemer, and this gave him steadfastness and constancy, though every other dependence, particularly the pride and boast of a self-righteous spirit, was tried and consumed. Another great doctrine of the faith, particularly set forth in the book of Job, is that of providence. It is plain, from this history that the Lord watched over his servant Job with the affection of a wise and loving father.

AUTHOR: Unknown

APPROXIMATE DATE: Unknown

THEME: Why Do the Righteous Suffer?

MAJOR CONTENTS
1. Job and the setting introduced (1:1 - 2:10)
2. Job is tested (1-2)
3. Job is consoled by his so-called friends (2:11 - 37:24)
4. God intervenes for Job (38-41)
5. Job repents and is restored. Job blessed with twice as much as he had (42)

SCRIPTURE MEMORIZATION

Job 1:1 describes Job as being a "Perfect" and _____ man. Job lived in the land of _____.

Job 1:21: And said, _____ came I out of my mother's womb, and naked shall I return thither: the Lord _____, and the Lord hath taken away; blessed be the name of the Lord.

Job 42:10: And the Lord turned the _____of Job, when he _____ for his friends: also the Lord gave Job _____ as much as he had before.

PSALMS

Psalms is the longest book in the Bible. It has the most chapters but Jeremiah has the most words. The book of Psalms, the hymnal of the Jewish people, is the Old Testament book most frequently quoted in the New Testament. Reading the book of psalms straight through is like reading a book of devotion, consisting of prayers and praises. The Psalms are lyric poetry, which is seen in that they appear in measured lines and are intrinsically fitted for song. Hold your Bible in your hand and turn to the middle of the book and you will find Psalms. Psalms 119 is the longest chapter in the Bible and Psalms 117 is the shortest chapter in the Bible.

AUTHOR(S): Mostly David along with a few other authors.

APPROXIMATE DATE: Compiled Fifth Century B.C.

THEME: Poetry

SCRIPTURE MEMORIZATION

Psa 27:1: The Lord is my _____ and my _____; whom shall I _____ the Lord is the _____ of my life; of whom shall I be afraid?

Psa 29:2: Give unto the Lord the _____due unto his name; _____ the Lord in the beauty of holiness.

Psa 30:5: For his _____ endureth but a moment; in his favor is _____: weeping may endure for a _____, but joy cometh in the morning.

Psa 103:12: As _____as the east is from the west, so far hath he _____ our transgressions from us.

Psa 119:11: Thy _____ have I hid in mine _____, that I might not sin against thee.

Psa 150:6: Let everything that hath _____ praise the Lord. Praise ye the Lord.

PROVERBS

Proverbs is the most practical book in the Bible. The first seven chapters read like the written advice of a father to a son. The rest of the book is a series of short principles concerning life and wisdom.

AUTHOR: Mostly Solomon with a few other authors.

APPROXIMATE DATE: Since Solomon is given the most significant role in the book, most of the proverbs would have been collected during the tenth century B.C. Hezekiah's men (25:1) compiled and edited it from 729-686 B.C.

THEME: Practical Wisdom: The author clearly sets forth his purpose to impart wisdom and understanding to all men

MAJOR CONTENTS
1. Introduction (1-9)
2. The Proverbs of Solomon (10:1 - 22:16)
3. Sayings of the wise (22:17 - 24:34)
4. Proverbs of Solomon which Hezekiah copied (25-29)
5. Words of Agur ben Jakeh (30)
6. Words of King Lemuel (31:1-9)
7. Praise of the ideal wife (31:10-31)

WHO CAN FIND A VIRTUOUS WOMAN? (PROVERBS 31:10-31)

PROVERBS

SCRIPTURE MEMORIZATION

Prov 1:7: The _____ of the Lord is the _____ of knowledge: but fools despise wisdom and instruction.

Prov 3:5-6: Trust in the Lord with all thine heart; and _____ not unto thine own understanding. In all thy ways _____ him, and he shall direct thy paths.

Prov 6:6-11: What insect does the Bible tell us to "consider her ways and be wise?" What do you learn from this scripture? _____

_____

Prov 16:7: When a man's ways _____ the Lord, he maketh even his _____ to be at peace with him.

Prov 16:25: There is a way that seemeth _____ unto a man, but the end thereof are the ways of _____.

Prov 18:10: The name of the Lord is a _____tower: the _____ runneth into it, and is safe.

Prov 18:21: Death and _____ are in the power of the _____: and they that love it shall eat the fruit thereof.

Prov 29:18: Where there is no _____, the people perish: but he that keepeth the law, _____is he.

ECCLESIASTES

Ecclesiastes describes many pursuits tried by the author to gain pleasure. Yet, they all ended up making him feel hollow, instead of satisfied. The general lesson of this book is that life is useless and empty without God. Ecclesiastes falls into two equal parts. The first six chapters establish the principle that all earthly things are futile and that the only way man can have personal satisfaction is to live in obedience to God. The last six chapters assume this premise and proceed to demonstrate that man can still reap earthly benefits regardless of environmental circumstances. Once man is led to see that earthly values cannot satisfy, he is ready for the conclusion of the book. "The Preacher" takes an accurate picture of life. He notices and records the selfishness, hypocrisy, greed, oppression, tyranny, ambition, and the social inequities of life. These things we share with him. He recognizes God's involvement with the world, the providential influence. However, the picture of God's dealings with men is somewhat unfocused. He declares that a definitive understanding of God's ways is not within man's grasp (8:17).

AUTHOR: Solomon

APPROXIMATE DATE: Tenth Century B.C.

THEME: The futility of life without God

MAJOR CONTENTS
1. Introduction (1:1-11)
2. The vanity and emptiness of all things without God (1:12 - 6:12)
3. Sayings on prudent behavior (7:1 - 12:7)
4. Epilogue (12:8-14)

SCRIPTURE MEMORIZATION

Eccl 9:11: The _____is not to the swift, nor the battle to the strong.

Eccl 12:13: Let us hear the _____ of the whole matter: Fear God, and keep his _____: for this is the whole duty of man.

SONG OF SOLOMON

Also known as "Song of Songs," this book describes the love between a man and a woman. The setting of the story is in Israel in the days of King Solomon. A maid of Shunem is fond of a young shepherd, but is taken by Solomon and placed in the harem in Jerusalem. Although Solomon tries to entice her with his wealth or advancement in the court, she remains faithful to the shepherd. Solomon finally realizes this and grants her permission to return home, which she does and is reunited with her lover.

AUTHOR: Solomon

APPROXIMATE DATE: Tenth Century B.C.

THEME: The Blessedness of Matrimonial Love: There is a threefold purpose to the book: (1) to honor the divine institution uniting one man and one woman, and to portray within that marriage conjugal love, especially in its romantic expression; and by analogy, (2) to show God's love for Israel; and (3) to illustrate the love of Christ for the church, i.e., that scarlet thread of redemption which runs through Scripture and which is illustrated most perfectly in the relationship between husband and wife (Eph. 5:25-33).

KEY VERSES: Love is as strong as death: The climax of the book, and therefore the key to the Song, is found in 8:6, 7, where the incredible power and value of love is described.

DID YOU KNOW?
The word "God" appears in every book of the Bible except Esther and Song of Solomon.

SCRIPTURE MEMORIZATION

Song of Solomon 8:6: Set me as a seal upon thine heart, as a seal upon thine arm: for love is

_____ as death; jealousy is cruel as the _____: the

coals thereof are coals of fire, which hath a most vehement flame.

POETRY - 05 BOOKS

APPLIED LEARNING PAGE

WHAT'S THE MISSING BOOK? _____

RECORD THE AUTHOR

JOB _____

PSALMS _____

PROVERBS _____

SONG OF SOLOMON _____

APPLICATION

Write a sentence or song using the first letters of each book to help you memorize the five books of poetry.

FUN LEARNING

Apply some of the fun learning techniques from the learning techniques page and repeat as needed.

APPLIED LEARNING PAGE

What book comes before Joshua? _____

What book comes before Nehemiah? _____

What book comes before Job? _____

What book comes before Proverbs? _____

Which TWO books in the Bible does not have God's name in them?

_____

_____

WRITE THE OT BOOKS OF LAW	WRITE THE OT HISTORY BOOKS	WRITE THE OT POETRY BOOKS

POETRY - 05 BOOKS
COURSEWORK

HOMEWORK ASSIGNMENTS

QUESTIONS I HAVE FOR A BIBLE TEACHER

SECTION SPECIAL NOTES

THE WORK OF A PROPHET

Usually people think of a prophet as one who foretells what is going to happen in the future. Prophets do some foretelling but as we study the Bible we learn that usually a Prophet warned the wicked. Their primary purpose was to warn and reprimand a sinful and unrepentant people to stop doing what they were doing before it was too late. They focused on the lack of morals in society which pointed to the sufferings of the day. Prophet means "One who speaks for another." Abraham was the first person called a prophet in the Bible (Genesis 20:7). Prophet is defined in Exodus 4:14-16 where Aaron was chosen to speak to the people for God, instead of his brother Moses. There are many Prophets and Prophetess in the Bible. To name just a few of the Prophetess, Miriam, was the first woman to be given the title of Prophetess (Exodus 15:20). Deborah, the Judge, was also a Prophetess (Judges 4:4). Huldah was a Prophetess (2 Kings 22:14 and 2 Chronicles 34:22); Noadiah was a Prophetess (Nehemiah 6:14); Anna was a Prophetess (Luke 2:36) and Phillip had four daughters who prophesied (Acts 21:9). Prophets of today must have the Holy Spirit before they can become a mouthpiece for God.

ROLES OF PROPHETS

✟ Could be men or women. Acts 2:17; Acts 21:8-9; Joel 2:28

✟ To be a mouthpiece for God and reveal His Divine purposes. Exodus 3:7-22; Exodus 4:10-17; Exodus 7:1-2; Jeremiah 1:4-19; Revelation 1:19

✟ To expose the enemy and his works. 2 Kings 6:8-23

✟ Sometimes to foretell. Amos 3:1-8; 2 Kings 17:18-23

✟ To guide and strengthen. 2 Chronicles 20:20-30; Revelation 12:17; Revelation 19:10; Revelation 14:12

✟ To call God's people to faithfulness. Malachi 4:5; 1 Kings 18

✟ To condemn sin. Exodus 5:1; Matthew 14:3-4

✟ To provide leadership. 1 Kings 18

✟ To teach and preach. Exodus 18:20; 1 Samuel 12:23; Mark 4:1; 6:2,34; Luke 11:1

✟ To pronounce God's judgments. Hosea 6:5

✟ To perform miracles. 2 Kings Chapters 4-6

✟ To execute judgment. 1 Kings 18:40

FALSE PROPHETS

Regarding False Prophets: Jeremiah 14:14; Jeremiah 23:16-32; Jeremiah 27:14-15; Jeremiah 28:15-17; 2 Chronicles 18:20-23; Matthew 7:15-18, Revelation 2:20.

THE MAJOR PROPHETS
05 BOOKS

ISAIAH

JEREMIAH

LAMENTATIONS

EZEKIEL

DANIEL

APPLICATION

Write a sentence or song using the first letters of each book to help you memorize the five Major Prophet books. One of my students, Aishah Ward, came up with the following saying:

EXAMPLE:

I	Just	Love	Eating	Donuts
Isaiah	Jeremiah	Lamentations	Ezekiel	Daniel

NOTE

The distinction between the Major and Minor Prophets is due to their length in writing rather than the Prophets "importance."

ISAIAH

Isaiah may be one of the more complicated books in the Bible to understand. Yet, it was the major prophet book most often quoted by Jesus. Isaiah prophesied during the reigns of the Judean kings (2 Kings.15-21). He was a citizen of Judah and the royal historiographer (2 Chr.26:22; 32:32). Assyria conquered and dismantled the northern Israelite kingdom King Ahaz became the "servant" of Tiglath-Pileser in exchange for the Assyrian conquest of Syria (2 Kgs.16:7-18). King Hezekiah rebelled against Assyria and trusted the Lord (2 Kgs.18 and19). The next Judean king, Manasseh, restored and increased idolatry and evil in Judah (2 Kgs.21) and the rest of the Judean kings, except for Josiah, tended to look to Egypt, rather than God. Prosperity and a period of peace served to deaden the people to the prophets' warnings about God's coming judgment. Isaiah foretold the coming judgment on Judah through Assyria and Babylon. He also looked ahead to the coming of God's Messiah and the final redemption of God's people.

AUTHOR: Isaiah: whose name means the Lord saves.

APPROXIMATE DATE: 700 B.C.

THEME: Judgment and Redemption

MAJOR CONTENTS
1. Prophecies of the ruin and restoration of Judah (1-5)
2. The call of Isaiah; biographical material (6-8)
3. The role of present world empires (9-12)
4. Prophecies regarding foreign nations (13-23)
5. Universal judgment and Israel's deliverance (24-27)
6. The moral indictment of the chosen people (28-31)
7. The restoration of the Davidic regime (32-33)
8. Judgment upon Edom and the restoration of the ransomed (34-35)
9. Biographical material from Hezekiah's time (36-39)
10. Prophetic assurances of comfort, deliverance, and judgment (40-45)
11. Declarations against Babylon (46-48)
12. Redemption through the work of the servant (49-55)
13. Ethical statements (56-59)
14. Life in the restored Zion (60-66)

ISAIAH

SCRIPTURE MEMORIZATION

Isa 1:18: Come now, and let us reason together, saith the Lord: though your _____ be as scarlet, they shall be as _____ as snow; though they be red like crimson, they shall be as wool.

Isa 26:3: Thou wilt keep him in _____ peace, whose mind is _____ on thee: because he trusteth in thee.

Isa 40:31: But they that _____ upon the LORD shall renew their _____; they shall mount up with wings as eagles; they shall run, and not be weary; and they shall walk, and not faint.

Isa 43:1-2: But now thus saith the Lord that _____ thee, O Jacob, and he that _____ thee, O Israel, Fear not: for I have redeemed thee, I have called thee by thy _____; thou art mine. When thou passest through the waters, I will be with thee; and through the rivers, they shall not _____ thee: when thou walkest through the fire, thou shalt not be _____; neither shall the flame kindle upon thee.

Isa 53:5: But he was _____ for our transgressions, he was _____ for our iniquities: the chastisement of our peace was upon him; and with his stripes we are_____.

Isa 54:17a: No _____ that is formed against thee shall prosper; and every _____ that shall rise against thee in judgment thou shalt condemn.

Isa 55:8: For my _____ are not your thoughts, neither are your _____ my ways, saith the Lord.

JEREMIAH

Jeremiah is the longest book in the Bible. It has the most words, even though it doesn't have the most chapters – as does the book of Psalms. The northern kingdom, Israel, had been gone for about a century. Despite reforms under Josiah, Judah continued to decline politically, spiritually, morally, and socially. Jeremiah prophesied during the final days of the Judean monarchy, as well as before, during, and after the Babylonian siege of Jerusalem. Jeremiah denounced sin and warned Judah of the rapidly approaching judgment. He also encouraged his brethren, foretold the coming Messianic prince, and the new covenant which God would make with Israel. Although opposed by a number of false prophets, Jeremiah foretold the coming siege of Jerusalem and captivity in Babylon through preaching, written material, and symbolic acts. He also sent a letter to those already in exile exhorting them to settle down and let God work out His plan.

AUTHOR: Jeremiah

APPROXIMATE DATE: Late Seventh Century B.C.

THEME: The Coming Judgment

MAJOR CONTENTS
1. Prophecies concerning Judah and Jerusalem (1-25)
2. Biographical material relating to Jeremiah's life and ministry (26-45)
3. Predictions against foreign nations (46-51)
4. Historical appendix (52)

SCRIPTURE MEMORIZATION
Jeremiah 1:4-8: Then the word of the Lord came unto me, saying, Before I formed thee in the _____ I knew thee; and before thou camest forth out of the womb I _____ thee, and I ordained thee a _____ unto the nations. Then said I, Ah, Lord GOD! Behold, I cannot speak: for I am a _____. But the Lord said unto me, Say not, I am a child: for thou shalt go to all that I shall send thee, and whatsoever I command thee thou shalt speak. Be not afraid of their faces: for I am with thee to deliver thee, saith the Lord.

Jeremiah 3:15: And I will give you _____ according to mine heart, which shall feed you with knowledge and _____.

Jeremiah 7:16: Therefore pray _____ thou for this people, neither lift up cry nor _____ for them, neither make intercession to me: for I will not _____ thee.

LAMENTATIONS

Lamentations is a series of five poems about Jerusalem after its capture by the Babylonians. It naturally follows the book of Jeremiah, where he told the people they would be destroyed if they didn't change their wicked ways, yet they refused to listen. Lamentations is Jeremiah's description of the suffering that had occurred as a result of the Babylonian siege.

AUTHOR: Jeremiah

APPROXIMATE DATE: 586 B.C.

THEME: The Destruction of Jerusalem: Lamentations is read annually in the land of Palestine to remind the Jewish people of their hour of deepest humiliation and grief, caused by their sin and guilt, which necessitated God's judgment. Furthermore, Lamentations enables the people to hope for the future deliverance which God has promised.

MAJOR CONTENTS
1. Jerusalem compared to a sorrowful widow (1)
2. Jerusalem's fall (2)
3. Some consolation found in God's mercy (3)
4. Horrors of the siege; the whole nation had sinned (4)
5. A prayer for deliverance and restoration (5)

SCRIPTURE MEMORIZATION

Lam 3:22-23: It is of the Lord's _____ that we are not

_____, because his compassions fail not. They are

_____ every morning: great is thy faithfulness.

EZEKIEL

Ezekiel, born during the optimistic reign of Josiah, grew up during the period of decline under Jehoahaz, Jehoiakim, and Jehoiachin. Daniel and others were taken to Babylon. More trouble brought the army of Nebuchadnezzar to Jerusalem again and Jehoiachin opened the gates of the city in submission to the Babylonians and 10,000 of Judah's leading citizens were taken as captives to Babylon. Ezekiel was among this large group of captives and continued to minister to his fellow-exiles in Babylon. Ezekiel's message is that God is faithful to His eternal purpose. He will punish the disobedient and preserve the faithful.

AUTHOR: Ezekiel means God strengthens

APPROXIMATE DATE: 593-571 B.C.

THEME: God's Holiness and Glory

MAJOR CONTENTS
1. Prophesy of condemnation spoken prior to Judah's fall in 586 (1-24)
2. Prophesy concerning foreign nations (25-32)
3. Prophesy concerning Israel's future restoration (33-48)

SCRIPTURE MEMORIZATION

Ezek 3:19: Yet if thou _____ the wicked, and he turn not from his wickedness, nor from his _____way, he shall die in his iniquity; but thou hast _____ thy soul.

Ezek 24:16-18: What sickness did Ezekiel's wife die from? _____

Ezek 36:26: A new _____ also will I give you, and a new _____ will I put within you: and I will take _____ the stony heart out of your flesh, and I will give you an heart of flesh.

Ezek 37:1-14: What do you learn from the vision of Ezekiel preaching in a valley full of dead bones?

_____

_____

EZEKIEL UNFORGETTABLE SERMONS

God asked the prophet Ezekiel to perform some unusual things in order to get the attention of the Israelite exiles. The following chart shows the meanings of these unusual "sermon illustrations."

PASSAGE	ACTIVITY	EXPLANATION
4:1–3	Writing on a clay tablet	Ezekiel used a clay tablet to sketch out a model depicting how Babylon would lay siege to Jerusalem.
4:4–8	Lying on his side	Ezekiel lay on his side to demonstrate that the length of Babylon's siege would correspond to the number of years Israel had sinned against God.
4:9–17	Baking bread over dung	Ezekiel baked his bread with a fire fueled by dung, which was offensive to the Jews. Ezekiel was illustrating that their captivity would force them to eat polluted food just like the filthiness of their sin.
5:1–4	Shaving his head	Ezekiel shaved his head as a sign of mourning. The burning of a third of his hair symbolized the fires that would destroy Jerusalem; the chopped hair stood for the people who would die by the sword; and the hair scattered in the wind represented those Jews who would be taken away into captivity.
12:1–16	Packing his bags	Demonstrated leaving Jerusalem to prepare the watching crowds for the coming exile of the citizens of Jerusalem.
12:17–28	Quivering	Trembling and shuddering while he ate, Ezekiel acted out the fear the Jews would encounter when their enemies swept through the land.
20:45–49	Preaching to the forest	Ezekiel preached toward the south in order to demonstrate that God would send judgment on Judah, the southern kingdom.
21:1–32	Preaching about a sword while sighing	Facing Jerusalem, Ezekiel used the picture of a sword to prophesy destruction. His deep sighs were intended to demonstrate the heavy hearts the people would have.
24:15–27	Refusing to mourn for his wife	God took Ezekiel's wife with a stroke as a sign of the overwhelming sadness the nation would feel when Jerusalem and the temple were destroyed.
37:1-4	Valley of Dry Bones	Ezekiel preached to the dry bones to show restoration of Israel.
37:15–28	Holding two sticks together	Ezekiel pictured the restoration of Israel by writing on one stick the name of Judah and on the other the name of Joseph, and then holding them together.

DANIEL

Daniel was among the selected "sons of Israel" who were taken to Babylon following Nebuchadnezzar's conquest of Jerusalem. In Babylon, Daniel was soon elevated to an honored place by the king who saw Daniel as a highly capable and trustworthy individual.

AUTHOR: Daniel

APPROXIMATE DATE: 530 B.C.

THEME: The Providence of God and the Last Days

MAJOR CONTENTS
1. Adjustments in Babylon (1)
2. Nebuchadnezzar's vision of four-sectioned statue (2)
3. Nebuchadnezzar's image and the three Hebrew boys in the furnace (3)
4. Nebuchadnezzar humbled (4)
5. Balshazzar's feast and Babylon's fall to Persia (5)
6. Daniel in the Lion's Den (6)
7. Prophecies of the future from Daniel's time (7-12)
8. Vision of the Four Beasts (7)
9. Vision of transition between Persia/Greece (8)
10. Appeal to return to Judah (9)
11. Daniel comforted (10)
12. Vision of Syrian/Egyptian struggles and final assurances (11-12)

SCRIPTURE MEMORIZATION

Dan 2:22: He revealeth the _____ and _____ things he knoweth what is in the _____, and the light dwelleth with him.

Dan 3:19: How many times hotter did Nebuchadnezzar make the furnace?_____

Dan 6:10: How many times did Daniel pray each day? _____

Learn why was Daniel cast into the lion's den? (Chapter 6) _____

_____

_____

THE MAJOR PROPHETS
05 BOOKS

APPLIED LEARNING PAGE

WHAT'S THE MISSING BOOK? _____

ISAIAH

JEREMIAH

EZEKIEL

DANIEL

<u>Note</u>

Each Major Prophet wrote the book bearing his name except Lamentations which was written by Jeremiah.

What's the difference between the Major and Minor Prophets?

_____
_____
_____
_____
_____

FUN LEARNING
Apply one of the fun learning techniques from the learning techniques page.

APPLIED LEARNING PAGE

What book comes before Job? _____

What book comes before Proverbs? _____

What book comes before Daniel? _____

What book comes before Isaiah? _____

WRITE THE OT BOOKS OF LAW	WRITE THE OT HISTORY BOOKS	WRITE THE OT POETRY BOOKS	WRITE THE OT MAJOR PROPHETS

THE MAJOR PROPHETS
COURSEWORK

HOMEWORK ASSIGNMENTS

QUESTIONS I HAVE FOR A BIBLE TEACHER

SECTION SPECIAL NOTES

THE MINOR PROPHETS
12 BOOKS

HOSEA

JOEL

AMOS

OBADIAH

JONAH

MICAH

NAHUM

HABAKKUK

ZEPHANIAH

HAGGAI

ZECHARIAH

MALACHI

HOSEA

The book of Hosea has a strange story line—the prophet is commanded by God to marry a prostitute. Hosea's ministry occurred within the span of years 755-715 B.C. The prophet must show Israel their unfaithfulness. Their idolatry is the sin they are charged with. God doesn't share His glory with another. He is God all by Himself. The prophet must show the ruin of the people, in the names given to his children. He foretells the fall of the royal family in the name of his first child: call his name Jezreel, which signifies "dispersion." He foretells God's abandoning the nation in the name of the second child; Lo-ruhamah, "not beloved," or "not having obtained mercy." God showed great mercy, but Israel abused his love. Sin turns away the mercy of God, even from Israel, his own professing people. The theme of Hosea's message is God's continuing love for an unfaithful people.

AUTHOR: Hosea: The name of Hosea means salvation.

APPROXIMATE DATE: 755-725 B.C

THEME: God's redeeming love for Israel which were considered the unfaithful people.

MAJOR CONTENTS
1. Parallel of faithlessness: the harlot wife, Gomer, compared to Israel (1:1 - 3:5)
2. Messages to unfaithful Israel (4:1-14:9)
3. Indictment for sin (4)
4. Warnings of judgment (8-10)
5. Israel's sin and final restoration (11-14)

SCRIPTURE MEMORIZATION

Hosea 1:2-3: What was the name of the prostitute Hosea married? _____

Hosea 4:6a: My people are _____for lack of knowledge.

JOEL

Through this prophet, God uses an analogy of a locust plague to warn the people of Jerusalem that judgment (through the Babylonians) is coming. A devastating locust plague and drought provided Joel with the opportunity to call Judah to repentance. He warned all of the inhabitants of the land of Israel of devastation which would sweep across the land in the days soon to come. He called for a season of fasting, mourning, and repentance.

AUTHOR: Joel: The name Joel means "Yahweh is God."

APPROXIMATE DATE: Ninth Century B.C.

THEME: Repentance and the Day of the Lord: Joel stressed repentance. He boldly censured the sins of the people and pointed to their need to repent.

MAJOR CONTENTS
1. A symbolic plague of locusts (1)
2. The day of the Lord symbolized (2)
3. Judgment of the nations (3)

SCRIPTURE MEMORIZATION

Joel 2:1: Blow ye the _____ in Zion, and sound an

_____ in my holy mountain: let all the inhabitants of the land tremble:

for the day of the Lord cometh, for it is nigh at hand.

Joel 2:21: Fear not, O land; be _____ and rejoice: for the Lord will

do _____ things.

AMOS

Amos is one of those minor prophet books that gives everyone an important weapon—the ability to recognize cults. Amos was born in Judah but prophesied in Israel during the reign of Jeroboam II. He condemned Israel's neighboring countries for their cruelty, but mostly Israel for breaking God's laws. He prophesied at Bethel which became the center of idol worship and the residence of king Jeroboam II. He warned that the Israelites would be taken captive by the Assyrians. Amos delivers God's warning of coming judgment on Israel and surrounding nations.

AUTHOR: Amos: The author's name means "burdened."

APPROXIMATE DATE: 760 B.C.

THEME: The Certainty of Judgment: Amos, a forerunner of three other outstanding eighth-century prophets -- Hosea, Micah, and Isaiah, etc. vigorously spoke messages on the certainty of judgment. Each message of judgment was not only a warning, but also a call to repentance.

MAJOR CONTENTS
1. Judgment against the nations (1-2)
2. The sin and punishment of Israel (3-6)
3. Five visions of the coming judgment (7:1 - 9:10)
4. Messianic blessing promised (9:11-15)

SCRIPTURE MEMORIZATION

Amos 3:3: Can two walk _____, except they be agreed?

Amos 5:14a: Seek _____, and not _____, that ye may _____.

Amos 8:11: Behold, the days come, saith the Lord GOD, that I will send a _____ in the land, not a famine of bread, nor a thirst for water, but of _____ the words of the Lord.

OBADIAH

Obadiah is the shortest minor prophet book. It contains only one chapter. It is also the shortest book in the Old Testament. It describes the future destruction of one of Israel's enemies, the ancient country of Edom. The conservative estimate of Obadiah's ministry places this oracle around 845 B.C. The central message is that Edom will be humbled and judgment is coming to all nations.

AUTHOR: Obadiah: The name "Obadiah" means "Servant of the Lord."

APPROXIMATE DATE: 586-539 B.C.

THEME: The Judgment of Edom: Its prophecy concerns the judgment of Edom for its treatment of Jerusalem. God is a God of moral justice; and He is in control, though events sometimes appear to indicate differently. Though God's people may be in trouble, they will one day be the recipients of God's blessings.

MAJOR CONTENTS
1. Edom's destruction predicted (1-9)
2. The cause of Edom's downfall: Malice against Israel (10-14)
3. The day of the Lord (15-21)

SCRIPTURE MEMORIZATION

Obadiah 1:15: For the day of the _____ is near upon all the

_____: as thou hast done, it shall be done unto thee: thy

_____shall return upon thine own head.

JONAH

Jonah contains one of the most widely recognized stories in Bible, that of Jonah being swallowed by a "large fish." Jonah was a native of Galilee. One day the Lord spoke to Jonah, son of Ammitai. He said, "Get up and go to the great city of Nineveh and denounce it because of the wickedness of the people. However, Jonah decided he didn't want to do what the Lord had commanded, and he headed in the opposite direction to Joppa. During his disobedience, the Lord sent a big fish to swallow Jonah, and he was inside the fish for three days and three nights. His miraculous deliverance from out of the fish rendered him a type of Lord.

AUTHOR: Jonah: This book has no stated author, though tradition ascribes it to Jonah, the main character of the book.

APPROXIMATE DATE: 800-750 B.C.

THEME: God's Mercy to Gentiles: The pervading theme of Jonah is God's gracious extension of His mercy to Gentile nations through the preaching of repentance.

MAJOR CONTENTS
1. Jonah's call and flight (1)
2. Jonah's prayer in distress (2)
3. Jonah's message brings Nineveh to repentance (3)
4. Jonah's displeasure at God's concern for the Gentiles (4)

SCRIPTURE MEMORIZATION

Jonah 1:2: Arise, go to _____, that great city, and cry against it; for

their _____ is come up before me.

Jonah 1:17: How many nights was Jonah inside the great fish? _____

Jonah 2:10: And the Lord spake unto the _____, and it vomited out

_____ upon the _____ land.

MICAH

Micah was raised up to support Isaiah, and to confirm his predictions. Micah insisted that the God of Israel and Judah expects His people "to do justly, to love mercy, and to walk humbly" with their God. Disobedience brings judgment. Nevertheless, Micah sees beyond the fall of Israel and the Exile of Judah to the incarnation of Christ and to the blessings of the millennial kingdom. As the prophecy ends, he marvels at the grace of the God who forgives. A very remarkable passage, Micah 5 contains a summary of prophecies that predicts the birth of Jesus in Bethlehem more than 700 years later.

AUTHOR: Micah meaning: "Who is like the Lord?"

APPROXIMATE DATE: 750-686 B.C.

THEME: Encouragement to Holy Living

MAJOR CONTENTS
1. The coming judgment upon the House of Israel (1)
2. The punishment and restoration of Israel (2)
3. Princes and Prophets condemned (3)
4. The future glory of the Kingdom (4-5)
5. Contrast of prophetic and popular religion (6)
6. Reproof of social corruption; promise of divine blessing (7)

SCRIPTURE MEMORIZATION

Micah 6:8: He hath showed thee, O man, what *is* good; and what doth the Lord require of

thee, but to do justly, and to love _____, and to walk

_____ with thy God?

NAHUM

Nahum is a book written to the people of Assyria and their capital of Nineveh. Nahum tells them their world empire will come to an end if they do not change their ways. They did not believe this prophet from the puny nation of Israel, and they were destroyed a hundred years later in 612 BC.

AUTHOR: Nahum

APPROXIMATE DATE: 650-620 B.C.

THEME: Nineveh's Approaching Destruction

MAJOR CONTENTS
1. A Psalm of God's majesty (1)
2. Description of Nineveh's destruction (2)
3. Reasons for Nineveh's destruction (3)

SCRIPTURE MEMORIZATION

Nahum 1:3: The Lord is _____ to anger, and great in power, and will not at all

acquit the wicked: the Lord hath his way in the whirlwind and in the _____,

and the clouds are the dust of his feet.

Nahum 1:7: The Lord is _____, a strong hold in the day of trouble; and he

_____ them that trust in him.

HABAKKUK

Habakkuk told the people in Judah (what was left of Israel in those days) to change their ways. Reacting like most people and nations to God's prophets, they told him to mind his own business. Habakkuk asked two questions that have long-plagued people. First, he wanted to know "Why does God allow wickedness to exist, especially in the midst of 'His people'?" (1:1-4). His second question (1:5-17) was "Why does God allow ungodly nations to arise and destroy other nations which don't appear to be as wicked as those which God uses to punish them?" Habakkuk 2:4"

AUTHOR: Habakkuk: The author of this book is Habakkuk, about who little is known apart from his name, which is derived from the Hebrew word meaning "embrace" or "embracer,"

APPROXIMATE DATE: 609-605 B.C.

THEME: Triumphant Faith: Realizing Israel's iniquity and need for punishment, Habakkuk is perplexed with the moral dilemma of how a Holy God could employ the more deplorably wicked Chaldeans to chastise His children. Habakkuk's theme is faith triumphant over apparent difficulties.

MAJOR CONTENTS
1. Complaint concerning unpunished lawlessness (1:2-4)
2. Oracle concerning the conquering Babylonians (1:5-11)
3. Habakkuk questions God's use of Babylon to punish Israel (1:12-17)
4. The wicked will be punished and the faithful will be saved (2:1-5)
5. Woes against the inhumanity of the Babylonians (2:6-20)
6. Habakkuk's prayer of faith (3)

SCRIPTURE MEMORIZATION

Hab 2:3: For the _____ is yet for an _____time, but at the end

it shall speak, and not lie: though it _____, wait for it; because it will

_____come, it will not tarry.

ZEPHANIAH

Zephaniah is another book warning the people in 6th century BC Judah that judgment was coming if they did not change their ways. Zephaniah prophesied during the reign of Josiah (640-609 B.C). King Josiah had inherited the legacy of moral and religious degeneration from Manasseh and Amon (2 Chronicles 33:1-25; 2 Kings 21:1-26). During Josiah's reign, a copy of the Mosaic Law was found in the Temple and sweeping reforms were made (2 Kings 22:1-23:25). Zephaniah's ministry preceded and helped to bring about these reforms. Zephaniah's message emphasized that God is still in control and will prove this through judgments on sinful nations.

AUTHOR: Zephaniah: The name Zephaniah literally means "Yahweh has treasured. The Lord is my secret."

APPROXIMATE DATE: 625 B.C.

THEME: The theme of the book is the necessity of seeking the Lord in view of the coming "day of the Lord" (1:7; 2:1-3)-the time of God's dire judgment upon the whole earth. The "day of the Lord" is an important concept in Scripture and is fundamental to a proper understanding of biblical eschatology. That "day" will begin with the rapture of the church, at the outset of the Tribulation period, and extend to the end of the Millennium and the melting of the elements of the universe (2 Peter 3:10-13).

MAJOR CONTENTS
1. The day of the Lord (1:1 - 2:3)
2. Judgments against foreign nations (2:4-15)
3. Woes and blessings (3)

SCRIPTURE MEMORIZATION

Zep 3:12: I will also _____ in the midst of thee an

_____ and _____ people, and they shall trust in the

name of the Lord.

HAGGAI

The Book of Haggai is the second shortest book in the Old Testament; only Obadiah is shorter. Haggai passes on God's message, encouraging his contemporaries to rebuild the temple in Jerusalem that was destroyed during the Babylonian conquest. It ties in nicely with the book of Ezra.

AUTHOR: Haggai. Little is known of the personal life of the prophet.

APPROXIMATE DATE: 520 B.C.

THEME: The remnant exhorted to be faithful: Israelite excitement over returning to the land was short-lived. Confronting them upon arrival was a city whose walls and houses had been reduced to debris overgrown with weeds. The temple in whose splendor they had taken pride and received recognition was nothing more than rubbish and ashes. Furthermore, there was drought in the land, and economic depression seemed imminent. Despite the odds, the returnees had set their hearts towards rebuilding, and shortly after their arrival the foundation of the temple was laid (Ezra 3:6-13). However, it seemed as though Yahweh had once more turned His face against the nation. Haggai's appeal to the people included an assurance that, despite the odds against it, God would guarantee the peace and prosperity of Jerusalem if the people would only be faithful to their responsibilities to Him.

MAJOR CONTENTS
1. Oracle challenging Judah to finish rebuilding the Temple (1)
2. Oracle encouraging faith in the second Temple's coming (2:1-9)
3. Oracle rebuking those who felt God's blessings were slow (2:10-19)
4. Oracle promising divine protection for Zerubbabel (2:20-23)

SCRIPTURE MEMORIZATION

Haggai 1:4: Is it time for you, O ye, to dwell in your _____ houses, and this

house lie _____?

ZECHARIAH

This book explains many symbols used in prophetic writing. It also refers to the restoration of the temple in Israel after the Babylonian conquest, tying in with the book of Haggai that precedes it. Finally, it contains many important prophecies regarding the coming Messiah—fulfilled 500 years later by Jesus Christ. God's message through Zechariah is for the people of Judah to "return to me and I will return to you" (1:3).

AUTHOR: Zechariah: The name Zechariah, a prevalent one in the Old Testament, means "the Lord (Yahweh) remembers."

APPROXIMATE DATE: 520-470 B.C.

THEME: Zechariah paints a picture of God's ultimate victory and the blessings to come to His faithful people through Messiah

MAJOR CONTENTS
1. Prophetic words of rebuilding the temple (1:1-8:23)
2. Series of night visions. (1:7-6:8)
3. Crowning of Joshua as the High Priest (6:9-15)
4. Fasting and social justice (9:1-11:17)
5. Prophetic words concerning Israel (9:1-14:21)

SCRIPTURE MEMORIZATION

Zechariah 13:7: Awake, O sword, against my shepherd, and against the man that is my fellow,

saith the Lord of hosts: smite the _____, and the _____

shall be scattered: and I will turn mine hand upon the little ones.

MALACHI

It had been 75-100 years since the Babylonian captivity had ended. The temple had been rebuilt and Judah was enjoying peace and prosperity under Persian rule. Judah's spiritual condition had declined. Malachi was concerned with the widespread indifference towards God in Judah. The priests were not faithful to their ministries and the people had not been taught God's word or proper reverence for Him. God declares that He has loved Israel by choice and has been faithful to His covenant. The people are challenged to repent and be faithful.

AUTHOR: Malachi: The name "Malachi" means "my messenger"

APPROXIMATE DATE: 435 B.C.

THEME: Encouragement to Covenant Faithfulness. Malachi instructs the people to renew their commitment to covenant faithfulness. He bases his command on Yahweh's demonstration of love for Israel (1:2), their spiritual and covenant unity with God and with one another (2:10), and the assurance of a coming day when the Lord will make evident the distinction between the obedient and the disobedient.

MAJOR CONTENTS
1. Decline of the priesthood and worship (1:1-2:9)
2. Sin in the family (2:10-16)
3. Coming forerunner, covenant and redeemed remnant (3:1-5)
4. God's faithfulness contrasted with Israel's unfaithfulness (3:6-18)
5. Messianic proclamation (4)

SCRIPTURE MEMORIZATION

Mal 3:8: Will a man _____ God? Yet ye have robbed me. But ye say, wherein

have we robbed thee? In _____and offerings.

THE MINOR PROPHETS
COURSEWORK

HOMEWORK ASSIGNMENTS

QUESTIONS I HAVE FOR A BIBLE TEACHER

SECTION SPECIAL NOTES

QUEENS OF THE OLD TESTAMENT

NAME	REFERENCE	IDENTIFICATION
Abijah	2 Kings 18:2	Mother of King Hezekiah of Judah
Athaliah	2 Kings 11	Evil daughter of Ahab and Jezebel; mother of King Ahaziah of Judah
Azubah	1 Kings 22:42	Mother of King Jehoshaphat of Judah
Bathsheba	2 Samuel 11-12 1 Kings 1-2	Wife of Uriah, then wife of David and mother of Solomon
Esther	Esther 2-9	Jewish wife of King Ahasuerus of Persia
Hamutal	2 Kings 23:31 2 Kings 24:18	Mother of King Jehoahaz and King Zedekiah of Judah
Hephzibah	2 Kings 21:1	Mother of King Manasseh of Judah
Jecoliah	2 Kings 15:2	Mother of King Azariah of Judah
Jedidah	2 Kings 22:1	Mother of King Josiah of Judah
Jehoaddin	2 Kings 14:2	Mother of King Amaziah of Judah
Jezebel	1 Kings 16:31; 18:13-19; 19:1-2; 21:1-25 2 Kings 9:30-37	Evil wife of King Ahab of Israel (who promoted Baal worship, persecuted God's prophets, and planned Naboth's murder)
Maacah	1 Kings 15:10 2 Chronicles 15:16	Mother of King Abijah and grandmother of King Asa of Judah
Meshullemeth	2 Kings 21:19	Mother of King Amon of Judah
Michal	1 Samuel 18:20-28; 25:44; 2 Samuel 3:13-16; 6:20-23	Daughter of Saul and first wife of David
Naamah	1 Kings 14:21-31	Mother of King Rehoboam of Judah
Nehushta	2 Kings 24:8	Mother of King Jehoiachin of Judah
Queen of Sheba	1 Kings 10:1-13	Foreign queen who visited Solomon to confirm his wisdom and riches
Zebidah	2 Kings 23:36	Mother of King Jehoiakim of Judah

THE MINOR PROPHETS
12 BOOKS

APPLIED LEARNING PAGE

WHAT'S THE MISSING BOOK? _____

Hosea
Joel
Amos
Obadiah
Jonah
Nahum
Habakkuk
Zephaniah
Haggai
Zechariah
Malachi

Note: Each of the Minor Prophet books was written by the Prophet whose book bears his name.

APPLICATION
Write a sentence or song using the first letters of each book to help you memorize the Minor Prophet books.

EXAMPLE:	**I**	**J**ust	**L**ove	**E**ating	**D**onuts
Major Prophets	**I**saiah	**J**eremiah	**L**amentations	**E**zekiel	**D**aniel

What's the shortest Minor Prophet book? _____

Which book does God command the Prophet to marry a prostitute? _____

Which book helps identify 'cults'? _____

FUN LEARNING
Apply one of the fun learning techniques from the learning techniques page.

APPLIED LEARNING PAGE

WRITE THE MAJOR PROPHET BOOKS	WRITE THE MINOR PROPHET BOOKS

OLD TESTAMENT
MINOR PROPHETS

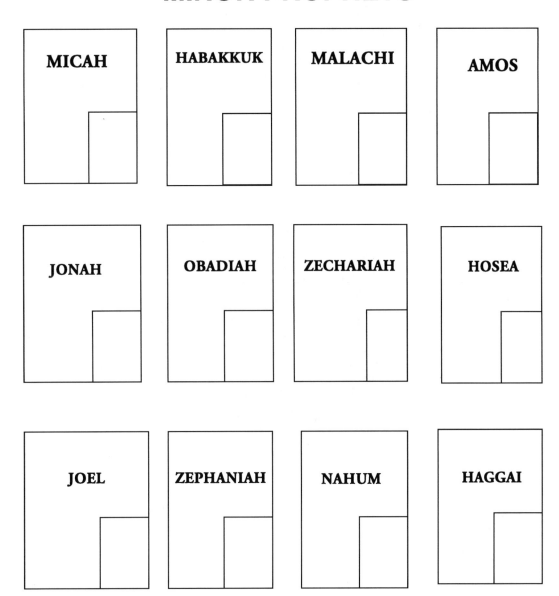

MICAH

HABAKKUK

MALACHI

AMOS

JONAH

OBADIAH

ZECHARIAH

HOSEA

JOEL

ZEPHANIAH

NAHUM

HAGGAI

RIGHT A NUMBER ON THE 12 MINOR PROPHET BOOKS IN THE PROPER SEQUENCE

FIND THE MISSING BOOKS
WORKSHEET

Record the TWO (2) missing books

_____

_____

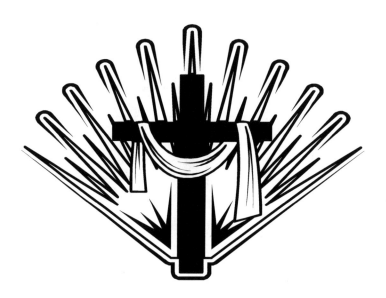

Isaiah
Jeremiah
Lamentations
Ezekiel
Daniel
Hosea
Joel
Amos

Obadiah
Jonah
Micah
Habakkuk
Haggai
Zechariah
Malachi

APPLIED LEARNING PAGE

By now you know the books of the LAW and therefore you will NOT be writing them down on this page.

WRITE THE OT HISTORY BOOKS	WRITE THE OT POETRY BOOKS	WRITE THE OT MAJOR PROPHETS	WRITE THE OT MINOR PROPHETS
Start with Joshua			

How many books are in the Old Testament? _____

Who wrote the majority of the Old Testament books? _____

What language was the OT originally written in? _____

Which two Bible books are named after women? _____

Record the three (3) OT books written by Solomon? _____

_____

_____

OLD TESTAMENT BOOKS
WORD SEARCH

You may consider using this for classroom studies. Set-up different teams and discover which team finds the most books within 10-15 minutes. This is a great tool for team building.

```
H E P V Z H Z G K Y C N K S Z S B R E V O R P O P
O A Z S Y E U I U N M V R N E J U T N V U S C S D
B E I E A R P V K K Y O U O C L V D V X I X D A S
A S D M K L R H K Y J S N M H G O U O S X E N E K
D O Z Y E I M D A L E O J O A U Z D E X C I L R N
I H J A X R E S B N T G I L R D V N U C E C O E C
A H R E T G E L A O I U M O I E E L L I T H Y M
H B W I A Q B J H I L A E S A G T E D N I E F A D
S N O I T A T N E M A L H G H T S U O B M L L J M
Q L F L R Z X Y W N E U T N C I H R E I N A F L P
G U S X F Q N E T F B Y P O A A H N A D C A W Q I
B M K L T K X Z R B R W S S N C M H Z H I F H R T
H Z Q J L R A R Z L L A T O K X W G I E J M Y U Z
S E S T H E R A U A I E J H V H M F D F E T X L M
D G D B R D L D K B S I U Z J Z P L J W M A F E W
E I N M I C A H W X L R P R P C T W D O U T E U M
V A B I W T L T D Z V O A R W H P A C H D W C M H
O Y C Z K S A P K U Z J L X A C A E S P P R R A R
T H K I K R S N C H X Y B Z T E F O I Z G U A S W
Z U F E P J O I U D E N E N A O J O S W T O O B C
I A G G A H W V A E W C N Z X A Z G A H K B U B C
Z E V J Q N U M B E R S E G D U J R I B U O J Z A
L E V I T I C U S R U R O E N I F O A M G J D Z F
M K R Z C G G W M B Y N P M Q T X L H N F I U V K
V J C W U W Q C Q T W G C T A Y Z J B Y M T O V A
```

AMOS	CHRONICLES	DANIEL
DEUTERONOMY	ECCLESIASTES	ESTHER
EXODUS	EZEKIEL	EZRA
GENESIS	HABAKKUK	HAGGAI
HOSEA	ISAIAH	JEREMIAH
JOB	JOEL	JONAH
JOSHUA	JUDGES	KINGS
LAMENTATIONS	LEVITICUS	MALACHI
MICAH	NAHUM	NEHEMIAH
NUMBERS	OBADIAH	PROVERBS
PSALMS	RUTH	SAMUEL
SONGSOLOMON	ZECHARIAH	ZEPHANIAH

FIND THE MISSING BOOKS
WORKSHEET

Record the THREE (3) Missing Books

_____

_____

_____

Genesis	Song of Solomon
Exodus	Isaiah
Leviticus	Jeremiah
Deuteronomy	Lamentations
Joshua	Ezekiel
Judges	Daniel
1 Samuel	Hosea
2 Samuel	Joel
1 Kings	Amos
2 Kings	Obadiah
1 Chronicles	Jonah
2 Chronicles	Micah
Ezra	Nahum
Esther	Habakkuk
Job	Zephaniah
Psalms	Haggai
Proverbs	Zechariah
Ecclesiastes	Malachi

Determine which are the missing books and check your answers with the index of your Bible.

OLD TESTAMENT BOOKS
WORD SEARCH

You may consider using this for classroom studies. Set-up different teams and discover which team finds the most books within 10-15 minutes. This is a great tool for team building.

```
G  U  P  Y  P  S  A  L  M  S  E  G  D  U  J
D  E  U  T  E  R  O  N  O  M  Y  O  G  O  O
E  H  N  J  E  R  E  M  I  A  H  M  B  A  S
Z  A  E  E  X  O  D  U  S  O  M  I  P  T  H
E  B  H  M  S  I  S  A  I  A  H  C  S  P  U
K  A  E  W  L  I  S  W  A  R  A  A  W  M  A
I  K  M  S  M  I  S  K  A  P  I  H  I  S  S
E  K  I  S  T  H  N  H  Z  S  S  X  A  U  B
L  U  A  K  A  H  C  U  E  Q  O  A  G  C  R
L  K  H  N  E  Z  E  L  X  U  M  M  G  I  E
E  H  O  Z  W  O  C  R  M  R  A  P  A  T  V
U  J  O  E  L  C  A  E  S  O  H  R  H  I  O
M  A  N  O  E  D  A  N  I  E  L  A  Z  V  R
A  C  H  R  O  N  I  C  L  E  S  N  F  E  P
S  R  E  B  M  U  N  K  I  N  G  S  E  L  O
```

WORD LIST

Genesis - Exodus - Leviticus - Numbers - Deuteronomy - Joshua Judges - Samuel - Kings - Chronicles - Ezra - Nehemiah - Esther Job - Psalms - Proverbs - Isaiah - Jeremiah - Ezekiel - Daniel - Hosea - Joel - Amos - Jonah - Micah - Habakkuk - Haggai

Who wrote the book of Ruth? _____

Who wrote the book of Numbers? _____

Which book records the story of the Lion's Den? _____

Which book records the vision of the Dry Bones? _____

Which book records the rebuilding of the Jerusalem walls? _____

FIND THE MISSING BOOKS
WORKSHEET

Record the FOUR (4) Missing Books

_____

_____

_____

_____

Exodus
Leviticus
Numbers
Deuteronomy
Joshua
Judges
Ruth
1 Kings
2 Kings
1 Chronicles
2 Chronicles
Ezra
Nehemiah
Esther
Job
Psalms
Proverbs
Ecclesiastes

Song of Solomon
Isaiah
Jeremiah
Ezekiel
Daniel
Hosea
Joel
Amos
Obadiah
Jonah
Micah
Nahum
Habakkuk
Zephaniah
Haggai
Zechariah
Malachi

Determine which are the missing books and check your answers with the index of your Bible.

OLD TESTAMENT BOOKS
WORD SEARCH

```
F  S  P  Z  J  O  T  P  Y  V  H  J  O  B  D  F  Z  H  E  D
S  M  E  S  P  S  E  L  C  I  N  O  R  H  C  V  E  A  Z  V
R  D  E  G  A  H  O  J  W  E  K  I  S  G  S  L  P  I  L  K
E  S  Y  C  D  L  A  M  O  A  R  Z  E  E  I  R  H  D  A  Z
B  O  W  L  C  U  M  G  A  E  X  X  I  N  A  T  A  A  M  V
M  N  A  E  C  L  J  S  G  H  L  J  L  E  T  Z  N  B  E  W
U  G  U  I  T  X  E  R  O  A  Q  N  C  S  N  Z  I  O  N  H
N  O  H  K  X  Y  F  S  O  N  I  K  H  I  K  Z  A  E  T  A
M  F  S  E  U  H  A  C  I  M  N  G  W  S  M  L  H  I  A  I
U  S  O  Z  B  R  Q  W  H  A  I  M  E  R  E  J  L  V  T  R
H  O  J  E  O  L  E  U  M  A  S  G  L  K  R  Z  H  U  I  A
A  L  S  M  K  W  P  J  R  S  T  T  Q  E  C  E  F  J  O  H
N  O  U  P  U  J  M  U  H  B  B  J  E  B  I  F  H  B  N  C
Z  M  C  S  K  I  S  A  I  A  H  R  O  S  G  N  A  T  S  E
U  O  I  U  K  R  R  T  Z  Y  I  G  E  N  E  R  A  D  S  Z
Z  N  T  D  A  U  H  K  W  K  N  M  N  V  A  G  D  D  Q  E
H  Y  I  O  B  T  K  I  N  G  S  L  E  V  O  H  R  E  Q  X
U  F  V  X  A  H  Z  Y  Z  Z  S  W  Y  H  Y  R  M  S  J  I
V  P  E  E  H  G  I  A  L  J  Z  G  T  A  E  V  P  S  K  U
G  M  L  Y  M  O  N  O  R  E  T  U  E  D  G  N  Z  S  D  I
B  J  K  C  O  S  I  H  C  A  L  A  M  M  Z  D  K  A  C  T
```

WORD LIST

Genesis Exodus Leviticus Numbers Deuteronomy Joshua Judges Ruth Samuel
Kings Chronicles Ezra Nehemiah Esther Job Psalms Proverbs Ecclesiastes Song
of Solomon Isaiah Jeremiah Lamentations Ezekiel Daniel Hosea Joel Amos
Obadiah Jonah Micah Nahum Habakkuk Zephaniah Haggai Zechariah Malachi

FIND THE MISSING BOOKS
WORKSHEET

Record the THREE (3) Missing Books

_____

_____

_____

Genesis	Proverbs
Exodus	Ecclesiastes
Leviticus	Song of Solomon
Numbers	Isaiah
Deuteronomy	Jeremiah
Joshua	Lamentations
Ruth	Daniel
1 Samuel	Hosea
2 Samuel	Joel
1 Kings	Amos
2 Kings	Obadiah
1 Chronicles	Jonah
2 Chronicles	Nahum
Ezra	Habakkuk
Nehemiah	Zephaniah
Esther	Haggai
Job	Zechariah
Psalms	Malachi

Determine which are the missing books and check your answers with the index of your Bible.

FIND THE MISSING BOOKS
WORKSHEET

Record the THREE (3) missing books

_____

_____

_____

Genesis	Proverbs
Exodus	Song of Solomon
Leviticus	Isaiah
Numbers	Jeremiah
Deuteronomy	Lamentations
Joshua	Ezekiel
Judges	Daniel
Ruth	Hosea
1 Samuel	Joel
2 Samuel	Amos
1 Kings	Obadiah
2 Kings	Jonah
1 Chronicles	Micah
2 Chronicles	Nahum
Ezra	Habakkuk
Esther	Haggai
Job	Zechariah
Psalms	Malachi

Determine which are the missing books and check your answers with the index of your Bible.

OLD TESTAMENT
WHERE IS THE SCRIPTURE?

By now you should have memorized many of the assigned scriptures. Now write down the Book, Chapter and Verse.

Where there is no vision, the people perish: but he that keepeth the law, happy is he.

_____

If my people, which are called by my name, shall humble themselves, and pray, and seek my face, and turn from their wicked ways; then will I hear from heaven, and will forgive their sin, and will heal their land. _____

Let every thing that hath breath praise the Lord. Praise ye the Lord. _____

There is a way that seemeth right unto a man, but the end thereof are the ways of death.

_____

Come now, and let us reason together, saith the Lord: though your sins be as scarlet, they shall be as white as snow; though they be red like crimson, they shall be as wool.

_____

And I will give you pastors according to mine heart, which shall feed you with knowledge and understanding. _____

For I am the Lord that bringeth you up out of the land of Egypt, to be your God: ye shall therefore be holy, for I am holy. _____

But he was wounded for our transgressions; he was bruised for our iniquities: the chastisement of our peace was upon him; and with his stripes we are healed.

_____

Thy word have I hid in mine heart, that I might not sin against thee. _____

For the vision is yet for an appointed time, but at the end it shall speak, and not lie: though it tarry, wait for it; because it will surely come, it will not tarry.

_____

Awake, O sword, against my shepherd, and against the man that is my fellow, saith the Lord of hosts: smite the shepherd, and the sheep shall be scattered: and I will turn mine hand upon the little ones. _____

OLD TESTAMENT
WHERE IS THE SCRIPTURE?

By now you should have memorized many of the assigned scriptures. Now write down the Book, Chapter and Verse.

But as for you, ye thought evil against me; but God meant it unto good, to bring to pass, as it is this day, to save much people alive. _____

Trust in the Lord with all thine heart; and lean not unto thine own understanding. In all thy ways acknowledge him, and he shall direct thy paths. _____

Will a man rob God? Yet ye have robbed me. But ye say, wherein have we robbed thee? In tithes and offerings. _____

And the Lord turned the captivity of Job, when he prayed for his friends: also the Lord gave Job twice as much as he had before. _____

And the Lord said, I have surely seen the affliction of my people which are in Egypt, and have heard their cry by reason of their taskmasters; for I know their sorrows.

_____

The Lord is my light and my salvation; whom shall I fear? The Lord is the strength of my life; of whom shall I be afraid? _____

God is not a man, that he should lie; neither the son of man, that he should repent: hath he said, and shall he not do it? Or hath he spoken, and shall he not make it good.

_____

In those days there was no king in Israel, but every man did that which was right in his own eyes. _____

And said, Naked came I out of my mother's womb, and naked shall I return thither: the Lord gave, and the Lord hath taken away; blessed be the name of the Lord.

_____

Can two walk together, except they be agreed? _____

Jesus said unto him, Thou shalt love the Lord thy God with all thy heart, and with all thy soul, and with all thy mind. And thou shalt love the Lord thy God with all thine heart, and with all thy soul, and with all thy might. _____

OLD TESTAMENT
WHERE IS THE SCRIPTURE?

By now you should have memorized many of the assigned scriptures. Now write down the Book, Chapter and Verse.

The Lord is slow to anger, and great in power, and will not at all acquit the wicked: the Lord hath his way in the whirlwind and in the storm, and the clouds are the dust of his feet.

_____

And if it seems evil unto you to serve the Lord, choose you this day whom ye will serve; whether the gods which your fathers served that were on the other side of the flood, or the gods of the Amorites, in whose land ye dwell: but as for me and my house, we will serve the Lord. _____

So built we the wall; and all the wall was joined together unto the half thereof: for the people had a mind to work. _____

So that the priests could not stand to minister because of the cloud: for the glory of the Lord had filled the house of the Lord. _____

Blow ye the trumpet in Zion, and sound an alarm in my holy mountain: let all the inhabitants of the land tremble: for the day of the Lord cometh, for it is nigh at hand.

_____

And Ruth said, entreat me not to leave thee, or to return from following after thee: for whither thou goest, I will go; and where thou lodgest, I will lodge: thy people shall be my people, and thy God my God. _____

He revealeth the deep and secret things: he knoweth what is in the darkness, and the light dwelleth with him. _____

It is of the Lord's mercies that we are not consumed, because his compassions fail not. They are new every morning: great is thy faithfulness._____

The name of the Lord is a strong tower: the righteous runneth into it, and is safe.

_____

In those days was Hezekiah sick unto death. And the prophet Isaiah the son of Amoz came to him, and said unto him, thus saith the LORD, Set thine house in order; for thou shalt die, and not live. _____

Yet if thou warn the wicked and he turn not from his wickedness, nor from his wicked way, he shall die in his iniquity; but thou hast delivered thy soul. _____

Saying, Touch not mine anointed, and do my prophets no harm. _____

WHO IS JESUS
IN THE OLD TESTAMENT

In Genesis — He is the Creator God
In Exodus — He is the Redeemer
In Leviticus — He is your sanctification
In Numbers — He is your guide
In Deuteronomy — He is your teacher
In Joshua — He is the mighty conqueror
In Judges — He gives victory over enemies
In Ruth — He is your kinsman, your redeemer
In I Samuel — He is the root of Jesse
In 2 Samuel — He is the Son of David
In 1st and 2nd Kings — He is King of Kings and Lord of Lords
In 1st and 2nd Chronicles — He is your intercessor and High Priest
In Ezra — He is your temple, your house of worship
In Nehemiah — He is your mighty wall against your enemies
In Esther — He stands to deliver from your enemies
In Job — He is the arbitrator
In Psalms — He is your song
In Proverbs — He is your wisdom
In Ecclesiastes — He is your purpose, delivering you from vanity
In Song of Solomon — He is your lover, your Rose of Sharon
In Isaiah — He is the mighty counselor
In Jeremiah — He is your balm of Gilead
In Lamentations — He is the ever-faithful one
In Ezekiel — He is your wheel in the middle of a wheel
In Daniel — He is the ancient of days
In Hosea — He is your faithful lover
In Joel — He is your refuge, keeping you safe
In Amos — He is the husbandman
In Obadiah — He is Lord of the Kingdom
In Jonah — He is your salvation
In Micah — He is judge of the nation
In Nahum — He is the jealous God
In Habakkuk — He is the Holy One
In Zephaniah — He is the witness
In Haggai — He overthrows the enemies
In Zechariah — He is Lord of Hosts
In Malachi — He is the messenger

PAGAN GODS OF BIBLE TIMES

PAGAN GOD	DESCRIPTION	BIBLICAL REFERENCE
Ashtoreths	Baal's wife or female counterpart.	Judges 2:13
Bel	A god identified with Merodach, chief Babylonian god.	Isaiah 46:1
Chemosh	God of the Moabites and Ammonites.	Jeremiah 48:7-13
Chiun	A star-god, identified with Saturn.	Amos 5:26
Dagon	Chief Philistine god.	1 Samuel 5:2–7
Hermes	The Greek god of commerce and speed.	Acts 14:12-13
Merodach	Chief Babylonian god, connected with war. Also known as Marduk.	Jeremiah 50:2
Molech	Ammonite god connected with child sacrifice.	Leviticus 18:21
Nebo	Babylonian god of wisdom and arts.	Isaiah 46:1
Rimmon	Syrian god of rain.	2 Kings 5:18
Tammuz	Babylonian fertility god.	Ezekiel 8:14
Zeus	Chief Greek god.	Acts 14:12-13

APPLIED LEARNING PAGE

How many books are in the OT? _____

What Language was the OT originally written in? _____

What are the Five Sections of the Old Testament? _____

_____

_____

_____

_____

What book includes the story of the walls of Jericho? _____

What book includes the story of the Red Sea? _____

What book includes the story of the Lion's Den? _____

What book theme is "Why does the Righteous Suffer?" _____

What book includes the story of Noah's Ark? _____

What book includes the story of the rebuilding of the walls of Jerusalem? _____

What book speaks of the vision of the dry bones? _____

What book tells of the Tower of Babel? _____

What book tells of the Prophet who married a Prostitute? _____

What book includes the story of a person swallowed by a large fish? _____

Which book says bring you all the Tithes into the Storehouse? _____

Which book includes the story of the Creation? _____

Which two books have the 10 commandments? _____

Which book includes the saying: The Lord is my Shepherd? _____

APPLIED LEARNING PAGE
WHO WROTE IT?

Genesis _____

Exodus _____

Leviticus _____

Numbers _____

Deuteronomy _____

Joshua _____

Judges _____

Ruth _____

1 Samuel _____

2 Samuel _____

1 Kings _____

2 Kings _____

1 Chronicles _____

2 Chronicles _____

Ezra _____

Nehemiah _____

Esther _____

Job _____

Psalms _____

Proverbs _____

APPLIED LEARNING PAGE
WHO WROTE IT?

Ecclesiastes

Song of Solomon

Isaiah

Jeremiah

Lamentations

Ezekiel

Daniel

Hosea

Joel

Amos

Obadiah

Jonah

Micah

Nahum

Habakkuk

Zephaniah

Haggai

Zechariah

Malachi

THE FEASTS OF THE LORD

NAME	SCRIPTURE	TIME	PURPOSE	SIGNIFICANCE
1. PASSOVER	Ex 12:1-28 Ex 43-49 Lev 23:5 Num 28:16 Deut 16:1-8	The evening of the fourteenth day of the first month of the biblical year (March /April)	**1.** Commemorate Israel's deliverance from Egyptian bondage. **2.** To remind the children of Israel that God "passed over" their houses, i.e. spared the firstborn of the Israelites.	**1.** Christ is our Passover (John 1:29; 19:36; 1 Corinthians 5:7; 1 Peter 1:18-19). **2.** The Passover is the foundation for the Lord's Supper (Matthew 26:17-30; Mark 14:12-25; Luke 22:1-20). **3.** The Passover foreshadows the marriage supper of the Lamb (Matthew 26:29; Mark 14:25; Luke 22:16-18).
2. FEAST OF UNLEAVENED BREAD	Ex 12:15-39 Ex 13:3-10 Lev 23:6-8 Num 28:17-25 Deut 16:3-8	It began on the fifteenth day of the month and continued for one week March/April)	**1.** Commemorate the hardships of Israel's hurried flight from Egypt. **2.** The absence of leaven symbolized complete consecration and devotion to God.	**1.** Unleavened bread is a type of Christ (John 6:30-59; 1 Corinthians 11:24). **2.** Unleavened bread is a type for the church (1 Corinthians 5:7-8).
3.DAY OF FIRST FRUITS	Lev 23:9-14	On the day after the Sabbath of Passover week (March/April)	To dedicate and consecrate the first fruits of the barley harvest.	**1.** First fruits is a type of the bodily resurrection of Christ (1 Corinthians 15:20-23). **2.** First fruits is a assurance of the bodily resurrection of all believers (1 Corinthians 15:20-23; 1 Thessalonians 4:13-18). **3.** First fruits is a type of the consecration of the church.

THE FEASTS OF THE LORD

4. FEAST OF PENTECOST	Lev 23:15-22 Num 28:26-31 Deut 16:9-12	The day after the seventh Sabbath after the Day of the First fruits (May/June)	To dedicate and consecrate first fruits of the wheat harvest.	1. The outpouring of the Holy Spirit upon the church occurred on the day of Pentecost (Acts 2). 2. The two loaves, representative of the Jew and Gentile, contained leaven because sin is found within the church.
5. DAY OF TRUMPETS	Lev 23:23-25 Num 10:10 Num 29:1-6	The first day of the seventh month, the sabbatical month (Sept/Oct)	To usher in and consecrate the seventh month as the sabbatical month.	In the N.T. the blowing of the trumpet is associated with the return of our Lord (Matthew 24:31; 1 Corinthians 15:52; 1 Thessalonians 4:16).
6. DAY OF ATONEMENT	Lev 16 Lev 23:26-32 Num 29:7-11	The tenth day of the seventh month Sept/Oct)	To make annual atonement for the sins of the people.	The Day of Atonement finds its fulfillment in the crucifixion of Christ (Hebrews 9).
7. FEAST OF TABERNACLES	Lev 23:33-43 Num 29:12-38 Deut 16:13-17	The fifteenth through twenty-first of the seventh month, with an eighth day added as a climax to all the feasts (Sept/Oct)	1. To remember God's deliverance and protection during the wilderness wanderings. 2. To rejoice in the completion of the harvest.	The Feast of Tabernacles foreshadows the peace and prosperity of the millennial reign of Christ (Zechariah 14:16).

THE SILENT YEARS

Four Hundred (400) Silent years separated the 39 books of the Old Testament from the New Testament. From the close of the Old Testament to the Birth of Christ, over 400 years transpired when Israel had no prophet to reveal the message of God. As a result, these are called the "silent years."

NEW TESTAMENT -27 BOOKS

The New Testament was originally written in the Greek language. Learn the divisions and names of the New Testament books in order. There are 27 books in the New Testament. Learn the five sections of the New Testament by associating them with your five fingers.

GOSPEL	**04**
HISTORY	**01**
PAULINE EPISTLES	**13**
GENERAL EPISTLES	**08**
PROPHECY	**01**

APPLICATION

Write a sentence or song using the first letters of each section to help you memorize the five sections of the New Testament.

THE GOSPEL

The Gospel means the good news or glad tidings of the coming Kingdom of God, and salvation from sin and death through the Lord Jesus Christ. The New Testament contains the story of the earthly life and ministry of Jesus Christ.

WHY FOUR GOSPELS?				
Gospel	**Matthew**	**Mark**	**Luke**	**John**
Audience	Jews	Romans	Greeks	Greeks
Description of Jesus	Jesus is the Messiah-King who fulfills Old Testament prophecy and expectations.	Jesus is the suffering Servant who ministers to our needs.	Jesus is the Son of Man who came to save and minister to all people.	Jesus is the divine Son of God in whom we should believe to receive eternal life.
Key Verses	Matthew 1:1; 16:16; 20:28	Mark 1:1; 8:27; 10:45; 15:34	Luke 19:10	John 20:31

WHY FOUR GOSPELS?

WHAT IS A PARABLE?

A Parable is an earthly story with a Heavenly meaning.

KEY TERMS DEFINED

DISCIPLE
A Disciple is a follower of Christ. Followers of Christ were not called Christians until the founding of the church at Antioch (Acts 11:26). Before then, Christians were called Disciples.

ESSENES
Essenes viewed both the Sadducees and the Pharisees as corruptors of Jewish law. Many Essenes were celibate and viewed the world as a conflict between the spiritual (good) and the physical (bad). They were tremendously concerned with ritual purity.

PHARISEES
The Pharisees was Jesus' most vocal critics. Their insistence on ritual observance of the letter rather than the spirit of the law evoked strong rebuke by Jesus; who called them self righteous. They were a powerful religious and political group amongst the Jews who strictly observed the Jewish law. They often focused on 'outward' forms of righteousness more than 'inward'. Unlike the Sadducees, they believed in the resurrection of the dead.

PUBLICANS
A political office created by the Romans. The Publicans (e.g., Zacchaeus, Luke 19:2) were Tax collectors employed by the Roman government. Many of them greatly oppressed the people. Jews who were publicans were hated by other Jews.

SADDUCEES
The Sadducees were a small wealthy sect of Jews who opposed the Pharisees. They did not believe in the resurrection, angels, or spirits. They were enemies of Christ.

SAMARITANS
The Samaritans were a mixed race, descendents of Jews and gentiles brought in by the Assyrian king during Israel's captivity. Samaritans were despised by the Jews.

SCRIBES
The Scribes were men trained in writing skills and were used to record events and decisions. They interpreted the law, taught it to disciples, and were experts in cases where people were accused of breaking the Law of Moses. They were usually Pharisees.

SYNAGOGUE
The Synagogue was a Jewish place of worship.

THE TWELVE DISCIPLES

MATTHEW 10:2-4   **MARK 3:16-19**   **LUKE 6:13-16**   **ACTS 1:13-14**

SIMON: More generally known as **PETER,** the brother of Andrew, a fisherman from the Sea of Galilee. Considered to be the most impulsive of the group, and always ready to speak up.

ANDREW: He was active in bringing people to Jesus, including his brother Peter.

JAMES: James was the older brother of John. He was a fisherman and left his trade to immediately follow Jesus. James is considered to have been in the "inner circle" of apostles, having been present each time, with only John and Peter, at the Transfiguration (Matthew 17:1), the raising of Jairus' daughter (Mark 5:37-43), and in the garden of Gethsemane (Mark 14:33). James was the first martyr among the twelve apostles, having been "put to death with the sword" (Acts 12:2).

JOHN: John eventually became a very close disciple, and friend, of Jesus. Jesus' nickname for John and his brother James was "Boanerges" which means "Sons of Thunder." John and James had been fishing with their father Zebedee and left immediately to follow Jesus.

PHILIP: Philip was from Bethsaida, as were Andrew and Peter. He was eventually martyred, possibly at Hierapolis.

BARTHOLOMEW: He was one of the disciples to whom Jesus appeared at the sea of Tiberias after His resurrection. He was also a witness of the ascension. Bartholomew was also called **NATHANAEL.**

THOMAS: He was also called **DIDYMUS**. Not easily convinced, he was given the nickname "Doubting Thomas" because he wanted to actually see and touch Jesus after His resurrection.

THE TWELVE DISCIPLES

MATTHEW 10:2-4   **MARK 3:16-19**   **LUKE 6:13-16**   **ACTS 1:13-14**

MATTHEW: Formerly a tax-collector at Capernaum, he became one of the more prominent apostles that followed Jesus Christ. Matthew (Levi) father's name was Alphaeus. Therefore, Matthew could have been the brother of James. Matthew was the writer of the first Gospel book, Matthew.

JAMES: Known as James the son of Alphaeus. Distinguished from the other apostle James, the son of Zebedee, and from James the brother of Jesus by being identified as James the son of Alphaeus. Some suggest him to be called "James the Less" or "James the Younger."

THADDAEUS: Also known as **JUDAS** not the Judas of Iscariot.

SIMON THE ZEALOT: The Zealots were a nationalistic sect with very strong political views.

JUDAS ISCARIOT: He was appointed as the keeper of the disciples' money, which was kept together in a sack (John 13:29). Judas' greatest weakness ended up being money. Judas was once offended by Mary, the sister of Lazarus, for her "wasting" expensive perfume to anoint Jesus. He claimed that the perfume could have been sold and the money given to the poor, but he actually wanted it for himself. Eventually, he betrayed Jesus for 30 silver coins (Matthew 26:15). After the betrayal, Judas repented but it was too late. He tried to return the money, but the officials refused to take back the money. Judas threw the coins into the Temple and then went off and hanged himself (Matthew 27:5). The chief priests could not put the "blood money" into the treasury so they used it to buy "the potter's field", to bury strangers in.

MATTHIAS: To bring the number back up to twelve after Judas fell away, Matthias was chosen by the remaining eleven apostles. (Acts 1:26)

MATTHEW

Matthew is one of the four "biographies" of Jesus in the Bible. The original audience was the Jewish people.

AUTHOR: Matthew who was a tax collector. He was one of the original twelve disciples.

APPROXIMATE DATE: Before A.D. 70

THEME: Jesus as King of the Jews

MAJOR CONTENTS
1. The birth of Jesus (1:1-2:23)
2. The genealogy of the King (1:1-17)
3. A harlot was an ancestor of Christ (1:5)
4. The incarnation (1:18-25)
5. The visit of the wise men (2:1-12)
6. The flight to Egypt (2:12-23)
7. The Galilean ministry of the King (3:1-18:35)
8. The forerunner of Jesus (3:1-12)
9. The baptism of Jesus (3:13-17)
10. The temptation of Jesus (4:1-11)
11. The initial ministry of Jesus (4:12-25)
12. The sermon on the mount (5:1-7:29)
13. The miracles of authentication (8:1-9:38)
14. The commission of the twelve (10:1-42)
15. The question of John the Baptist (11:1-19)
16. Warnings (11:20-12:50)
17. The parables of the Kingdom (13:1-58)
18. The death of John the Baptist (14:1-12)
19. The miracles of providence (14:13-36)
20. Conflicts with religious authorities (15:1-16:12)
21. The confession of Peter (16:13-28)
22. The Transfiguration (17:1-13)
23. The continuing ministry in Galilee (17:14-27)
24. Principles for Kingdom relationships (18:1-35)
25. The Judean ministry of the King (19:1-20:34)
26. Questions concerning the family (19:1-15)
27. The approach of the rich young ruler (19:16-30)
28. The parable of the vineyard workers (20:1-19)
29. The request of Zebedee's wife (20:20-29)
30. The healing of two blind men (20:30-34)
31. The last days in Judea (21:1-27:66)
32. The triumphal entry (21:1-11)

33. The cleansing of the Temple (21:12-22)
34. The questions of authority (21:23-46)
35. The questions of theology (22:1-46)
36. Prophetic woes (23:1-39)
37. The fifth discourse (24:1-25:46)
38. The Passover and Last Supper (26:1-35)
39. The Garden of Gethsemane (26:36-46)
40. The betrayal and trial (26:47-27:25)
41. The scourging and crucifixion (27:26-66)
42. The concluding events and Great Commission (28:1-20)

The Royal Line to Christ

Boaz and Ruth

Obed

See Luke 3:32-38 for the generations from Boaz back to Adam.

Jesse

See Matthew 1:6-16 for the generations from David to Christ.

David

Christ

SCRIPTURE MEMORIZATION

Mat 3:13: Which river did John baptize Jesus in? _____

Mat 4: What did Jesus do to resist Satan's temptations? _____

Mat 4:4: But he answered and said, It is _____, Man shall not live by bread

alone, but by every _____ that proceedeth out of the mouth of God.

Mat 6:8: When we pray, does the Father know what we need before we even ask?

_____

Mat 6:33: But seek ye_____ the kingdom of God, and his _____;

and all these things shall be added unto you.

Mat 7:1: _____ not, that ye be not judged.

Mat 14:3-10: Who had John the Baptist beheaded? _____

Mat 18:22: How many times did Jesus say to forgive? _____

Mat 22:37-40: Jesus said unto him, Thou shalt love the Lord thy God with all thy

_____, and with all thy _____, and with all thy

_____. This is the first and great commandment. And the second is like unto it, Thou shalt love thy _____ as thyself. On these two commandments _____ all the law and the prophets.

Mat 26:14-15: Who accepted money to betray Jesus? _____

Mat 26:69-75: Who denied Jesus three times? _____

Mat 27:32: Who helped Jesus carry His cross? _____

THE GREAT COMMISSION

Jesus Christ left the church with a mandate to 'preach the gospel to every creature.' Along with this mandate, He also left us with the tools to achieve the job. He has given this task into the hands of men and women like you and me. Once you have accepted Jesus Christ, It is important for you to openly declare Jesus Christ as your Lord and Savior. Don't keep it a secret. God doesn't want anyone to be lost. The responsibility of spreading the Gospel to the world has been committed to all believers.

Matthew 28:19-20: Go ye therefore, and teach all nations, baptizing them in the _____ of the Father, and of the Son, and of the Holy Ghost: Teaching them to observe all things whatsoever I have _____ you and, lo, I am with you always, even unto the end of the world. Amen.

Matthew 4:18-19: And Jesus, walking by the sea of Galilee, saw two brethren, Simon called _____, and Andrew his brother, casting a net into the sea: for they were fishers. And he saith unto them, Follow me, and I will make you fishers of _____. And they straightway left their nets, and followed him.

Matthew 5 13-16: Ye are the _____ of the earth: but if the salt has lost his savour, wherewith shall it be salted? it is thenceforth good for nothing, but to be cast out, and to be trodden under foot of men. Ye are the _____ of the world. A city that is set on an hill cannot be hid. Neither do men light a candle, and put it under a bushel, but on a candlestick; and it giveth light unto all that are in the house. Let your light so shine before men, that they may see your good works, and glorify your _____ which is in Heaven.

MARK

Mark is the second of the four Biblical "biographies" of Jesus. More powerful in that it begins with the actual ministry of Jesus and quickly moves through the manifestation of the His earthly life. Mark or one of the other gospels is the recommended book in the Bible to start your studies.

AUTHOR: Mark

APPROXIMATE DATE: A.D. 65-68

THEME: Encouragement for Persecuted Believers: Mark's audience of Roman Christians found themselves facing bitter persecution. These Roman Christians needed to recognize that being a disciple of Jesus Christ is costly, but that they were facing no more than their Master had already faced for them.

MAJOR CONTENTS
1. The Messiah's preparation for ministry In the wilderness (1:1-13)
2. Introduction to the Gospel (1:1)
3. John the Baptist prepares the way to repentance (1:2-8)
4. The Messiah is baptized (1:9-11)
5. The Messiah is tempted (1:12-13)
6. The Messiah's Ministry (in and around Galilee) (1:14-8:30)
7. The Messiah's message: repent and believe (1:14-15)
8. The Messiah's men: Follow me (1:16-20)
9. The Messiah's authority (1:21-45)
10. The Messiah faces conflicts (2:1-3:6)
11. The Messiah's followers (3:7-19)
12. The Messiah encounters opposition (3:20-35)
13. The Messiah's ministry: parable teachings (4:1-34)
14. The Messiah's miracles (4:35-5:43)
15. The Messiah's rejection (6:1-6)
16. The Messiah's commission (6:7-13)
17. The Messiah's forerunner: His Death (6:14-29)
18. The Messiah's miracles and teaching (6:30-8:26)
19. Peter's confession (8:27-30)
20. First passion prediction (8:31-33)
21. First teaching on discipleship (8:34-9:29)
22. Second passion prediction (9:30-32)
23. Teaching on discipleship (9:33-10:31)
24. Third passion prediction (10:32-34)
25. Third teaching on discipleship (10:35-52)

26. The Messiah's ministry in Jerusalem (11:1-13:37)
27. Triumphal entry (11:1-11)
28. Judgment on Israel (11:12-26)
29. Conflict with the religious leaders (11:27-12:34)
30. Teaching in the Temple (12:35-44)
31. Be alert awaiting His return (13:1-37)
32. The crucifixion (14:1-15:47)
33. Plot conceived (14:1-2)
34. Anointing for burial (14:3-9)
35. Betrayed by Judas (14:10-11)
36. The Last Supper (14:12-26)
37. Denial predicted (14:27-31)
38. Agonizing prayer at Gethsemane (14:32-42)
39. The Arrest (14:43-52)
40. The Jewish trial: charged with blasphemy (14:53-65)
41. Denial was fulfilled (14:66-72)
42. The Roman trial (15:1-15)
43. The King is mocked (15:16-20)
44. The King is crucified (15:21-38)
45. The King is acknowledged (15:39)
46. The King is buried (15:40-47)
47. The Messiah's Resurrection (16:1-20)
48. The Women find an empty tomb (16:1-5)
49. The Angel's victorious announcement (16:6-7)
50. The women's fearful response (16:8)
51. Post-resurrection appearances of Jesus (16:9-13)
52. Commission of the disciples (16:14-18)
53. Ascension of Jesus (16:19-20)

SCRIPTURE MEMORIZATION

Mark 3:29: But he that shall _____ against the Holy Ghost hath never forgiveness, but is in _____ of eternal damnation.

Mark 4:9: And he said unto them, He that hath _____ to hear, let him _____.

Mark 5:22-24; 35:43: Whose daughter did Jesus raise from the dead? _____

Mark 6:4: But Jesus said unto them, a _____ is not without honor, but in his own _____, and among his own _____, and in his own _____.

Mark 11:1-7: What did Jesus ride on into Jerusalem? _____

LUKE

Luke is the longest of the four "biographies" of Jesus in the Bible. This is the book in the Bible that covers the birth of Jesus in more details. It also contains a story in chapter 16 that gives us a glimpse of heaven and hell.

AUTHOR: Luke, who was a physician

APPROXIMATE DATE: A.D. 59-61

THEME: Jesus Christ has come to save all

MAJOR CONTENTS
1. The infancy and early years of the Savior (1:5-2:52)
2. The annunciation of the birth of John the Baptist (1:5-25)
3. The annunciation of the birth of the Savior (1:26-38)
4. The visit of Mary to Elizabeth (1:39-56)
5. The birth of John the Baptist (1:57-80)
6. The birth of Jesus (2:1-20)
7. The circumcision, naming, and the Savior in the Temple (2:21-40)
8. The Savior's entrance into his work (3:1-4:13)
9. The ministry of John the Baptist (3:1-20)
10. The baptism of the Savior (3:21, 22)
11. The genealogy of the Savior (3:23-38)
12. The temptation of Jesus in the Wilderness (4:1-13)
13. Jesus as God's agent of Salvation (4:14-9:50)
14. The rejection at Nazareth (4:14-30)
15. The dawning of the new age (4:31-44)
16. The first disciples (5:1-11)
17. The struggle between the new and the old (5:12-6:11)
18. The new community of disciples (6:12-49)
19. Reaching out to others (7:1-8:3)
20. The itinerant ministry of Jesus (8:4-56)
21. The mission for His disciples (9:1-17)
22. Peter's great confession (9:18-21)
23. Foretelling His death (9:22-27)
24. The transfiguration of Jesus (9:28-36)
25. The future of the twelve disciples (9:37-50)
26. Revealing the meaning of discipleship (9:51-11:13)
27. The good Samaritan (10:29-37)
28. The Lord's prayer (11:2-4)

29. Israel's rejection of the Savior (11:14-13:17)
30. Teaching about the Kingdom (13:18-14:35)
31. The Prodigal son (15:1-32)
32. Teaching the duties of discipleship (16:1-17:19)
33. Watching for the Kingdom (17:20-18:34)
34. The Jericho road (18:35-19:27)
35. Jesus, Savior and Lord, triumphant in Jerusalem (19:28-24:53)
36. The enthusiasm of the crowds (19:28-38)
37. Pointing out the failures of Judaism (19:39-21:4)
38. Warnings about the future (21:5-36)
39. Summary of His days in Jerusalem (21:37-38)
40. Preparing for the cross and trial of Jesus (22:1-23:25)
41. The Crucifixion (23:26-56)
42. His Resurrection and Ascension (24:1-53)

SCRIPTURE MEMORIZATION

Luke 2:4-7: Where was Jesus born? _____

Luke 2:42: How old was Jesus when his parents found him in the temple? _____

Luke 10:29-37: Read about the Good Samaritan. Which two people passed by the wounded man? _____ and the _____ What did the Good Samaritan do for the wounded man? _____

_____

Luke 15:10: Likewise, I say unto you, there is _____ in the presence of the angels of God over _____ sinner that repenteth.

Luke 15: Read the story of the Prodigal (wasteful) son. What did the prodigal son eat after he lost all his money? What do you learn from this story?

_____

Luke 17:15: There were 10 lepers healed by Jesus. How many of the ten returned to say "Thank You" _____

Luke 19:10: For the Son of man is come to _____ and to _____that which was _____.

Luke 19:2-4: Who climbed the sycamore tree to see Jesus? _____

Luke 23:33: On what hill was Jesus crucified? _____

JOHN

John is the last of the four "biographies" of Jesus in the Bible. Different from the others, John opens his book with symbolism.

AUTHOR: John the Apostle

APPROXIMATE DATE: A.D. 80-95

THEME: Jesus as Son of God

MAJOR CONTENTS
1. The Prologue (1:1-18)
2. Pre-incarnate Word (1:1-5)
3. The Incarnate Word (1:6-18)
4. The presentation (1:19-51)
5. Written to the Jewish leaders from Jerusalem (1:19-34)
6. Written to the first disciples (1:35-51)
7. Public ministry in signs and discourses (2:1-12:50)
8. The first miracle: changing water into wine (2:1-12)
9. Cleansing the Temple (2:13-25)
10. The new birth (3:1-21)
11. The ministry in the Judean country side (3:22-4:4)
12. The ministry in Samaria (4:5-42)
13. The second miracle: Healing the Nobleman's son in Galilee (4:43-54)
14. The third miracle: Healing the Paralytic (5:1-47)
15. The activity by the sea of Galilee (6:1-71)
16. The activity at the Feast of Tabernacles (7:1-52)
17. The light of the world (7:53-8:59)
18. The miracle of giving sight to the blind (9:1-41)
19. The good Shepherd (10:1-42)
20. Raising of Lazarus (11:1-53)
21. Isolation in Ephraim (11:54-57)
22. The closing events of the public ministry (12:1-50)
23. The private ministry to the disciples (13:1-16:33)
24. The events in the upper room (13:1-14:31)
25. The final discourses (15:1-16:33)
26. The Pastoral prayer (17:1-26)
27. The passion and resurrection (18:1-20:10)
28. Jesus betrayal and arrest (18:1-14)
29. The trials and the denials of Peter (18:15-19:16)
30. Jesus crucifixion and burial (19:16-42)

31. The resurrection (20:1-10)
32. The post-resurrection ministry (20:11-21:23)
33. Jesus various appearances (20:11-29)
34. The writer's purpose (20:30-31)
35. The miracle: Great catch of fish (21:1-14)
36. The restoration of Peter (21:15-19)
37. The beloved disciple (21:20-23)

SCRIPTURE MEMORIZATION

John 1:1: In the beginning was the _____, and the _____ was with God, and the Word was God.

John 2:9: What did Jesus turn into wine? _____

John 3:1-2: Who came to Jesus at night to ask about salvation? _____

John 3:16-17: For God so loved the world, that he gave his only_____ Son, that _____ believeth in him should not perish, but have everlasting life. For God sent not his Son into the world to _____ the world; but that the world through him might be_____.

John 5:2-3: Which pool of Jerusalem was used for healing the sick? _____

John 7:24: Judge not according to the _____, but judge _____ judgment.

John 9:6: What did Jesus use to heal a blind man? _____

John 11:17: How many days was Lazarus dead? _____

John 11:35: What is the shortest verse in the Bible? _____

John 12:32: And I, if I be _____ up from the earth, will _____ all men unto me.

John 13:8: What disciple, at first, didn't want Jesus to wash his feet? _____

John 15:16: Ye have not _____ me, but I have chosen you, and _____ you, that ye should go and bring forth fruit, and that your fruit should remain: that whatsoever ye shall ask of the Father in my name, he may give it you.

John 18:10: What did Peter do to the high priest's servant after Jesus was betrayed?

_____

John 20:27: Which disciple at first doubted the resurrection of Jesus? _____

THE SEVEN 'I AM' SAYINGS OF JESUS

1. BREAD
And Jesus said unto them, **I am the bread of life**: he that cometh to me shall never hunger; and he that believeth on me shall never thirst. (John 6:35)

2. LIGHT
Then spake Jesus again unto them, saying, **I am the light** of the world: he that followeth me shall not walk in darkness, but shall have the light of life. (John 8:12)

3. DOOR
I am the door: by me if any man enter in, he shall be saved, and shall go in and out, and find pasture. (John 10:9)

4. GOOD SHEPHERD
I am **the good shepherd**: the good shepherd giveth his life for the sheep. (John 10:11)

5. RESURRECTION AND LIFE
Jesus said unto her, **I am the resurrection**, and **the life**: he that believeth in me, though he were dead, yet shall he live. (John 11:25)

6. WAY, TRUTH, LIFE
Jesus saith unto him, **I am the way, the truth, and the life**: no man cometh unto the Father, but by me. (John 14:6)

7. TRUE VINE
I am **the true vine**, and my Father is the husbandman. (John 15:1)

THE MIRACLES OF JESUS

1.	The water changed into wine	John 2:1-11
2.	Healing of a nobleman's son	John 4:46-54
3.	Healing of a sick man	John 5:1-9
4.	Healing of a man who was born blind	John 9:1-41
5.	Raising of Lazarus	John 11:1-44
6.	The hundred and fifty three fish	John 21:1-11
7.	Walking on the sea	John 6:19-21
8.	Feeding five thousand hungry people	John 6:5-13
9.	Freeing a man's soul which was possessed by demons	Luke 4:33-35
10.	Healing of Simon's mother in law	Luke 4:38-39
11.	The great catch of fish	Luke 5:1-11
12.	Healing of a leper	Luke 5:12-13
13.	Healing of a man who was paralyzed	Luke 5:18-25
14.	The restoration of the withered hand	Luke 6:6-10
15.	Healing of a centurion's slave	Luke 7:1-10
16.	The raising of a widow's son	Luke 7:11-15
17.	The storm	Luke 8:22-25
18.	Freeing Legions from the evil spirits	Luke 8:27-35
19.	Healing of Jairus' daughter	Luke 8:41-56
20.	Healing of a woman with issue of blood	Luke 8:43-48
21.	Freeing a boy's soul which was seized by demons	Luke 9:38-43
22.	Healing a dumb demon possessed man	Luke 11:14
23.	Healing a crippled woman	Luke 13:11-13
24.	Healing a man with dropsy	Luke 14:1-4
25.	Healing ten lepers	Luke 17:11-19
26.	Healing of a blind man	Luke 18:35-43
27.	Healing of a slave's ear	Luke 22:50-51
28.	Healing of two blind men	Mat 9:27-31
29.	Healing of a dumb demon possessed man	Mat 9:32-33
30.	Healing of the Canaanite girl who was seized by demons	Mat 15:21-28
31.	Feeding four thousand hungry people	Mat 15:32-38
32.	The money in the fish's mouth	Mat 17:24-27
33.	The withering of the fig tree	Mat 21:18-22
34.	Healing a deaf and mute man	Mark 7:31-37
35.	Healing a blind man	Mark 8:2-26

PARABLES OF JESUS CHRIST

	PARABLE	MATTHEW	MARK	LUKE
1	Lamp under a Basket	5:14-16	4:21-22	8:16-17
				11:33-36
2	A Wise Man Builds on Rock	7:24-27		6:47-49
3	New Cloth on and Old Garment	9:16	2:21	5:36
4	New Wine in Old Wineskins	9:17	2:22	5:37-38
5	The Sower	13:3-23	4:2-20	8:4-15
6	The Tares (Weeds)	13:24-30		
7	The Mustard Seed	13:31-32	4:30-32	13:18-19
8	The Leaven	13:33		13:20-21
9	The Hidden Treasure	13:44		
10	The Pearl of Great Price	13:45-46		
11	The Dragnet	13:47-50		
12	The Householder	13:52		
13	The Lost Sheep	18:12-14		15:3-7
14	The Unforgiving Servant	18:23-35		
15	The Workers in the Vineyard	20:1-16		
16	The Two Sons	21:28-32	12:1-12	
17	The Wicked Tenants	21:33-45		20:9-19
18	The Wedding Feast	22:2-14	13:28-32	14:16-24
19	The Fig Tree	24:32-44		21:29-33
20	The Ten Virgins	25:1-13		
21	The Talents	25:14-30	4:26-29	
22	The Growing Seed		13:33-37	
23	The Watchful Porter			
24	The Creditor and Two Debtors			7:41-43
25	The Good Samaritan			10:30-37
26	A Friend in Need			11:5-13
27	The Rich Fool			12:16-21
28	The Faithful and Wise Servant			12:35-40
29	Faithful and Wicked Steward	24:45-51		12:42-48
30	The Barren Fig Tree			13:6-9
31	The Lowest Seat			14:7-11
32	Building a Tower and Making War			14:25-35
33	The Lost Coin			15:8-10
34	The Lost Son			15:11-32
35	The Shrewd Manager			16:1-13
36	The Rich Man and Lazarus			16:19-31
37	Unprofitable Servants			17:7-10
38	The Persistent Widow			18:1-8
39	The Pharisee and the Tax Collector			18:9-14
40	The Minas (Pounds)			19:11-27

THE MIRACLES OF
PETER AND PAUL

PETER

Acts 2:37-41	Day of Pentecost sermon led 3,000 to salvation
Acts 3:1-11	Was used to heal a man lame from birth
Acts 5:15-16	Peter's shadow healed people
Acts 5:17	Success caused Jewish jealousy
Acts 8:9-24	Dealt with Simon, a sorcerer
Acts 9:36-41	Was used to raise Dorcas to life

PAUL

Acts 14:8-18	Was used to heal a man lame from birth
Acts 19:11-12	Handkerchiefs and aprons from Paul healed people
Acts 13:45	Success caused Jewish jealousy
Acts 13:6-11	Dealt with Bar-Jesus, a sorcerer
Acts 20:9-12	Was used to raise Eutychus to life

NEW TESTAMENT WOMEN

NAME	DESCRIPTION	SCRIPTURE
Mary	The virgin mother of Jesus. She is an enduring example of faith, humility, and service.	Luke 1:26-56
Anna	Recognized Jesus as the long-awaited Messiah.	Luke 2:36-38
Bernice	Sister of Agrippa before whom Paul made his defense.	Acts 25:13
Candace	A queen of Ethiopia.	Acts 8:27
Chloe	Woman who knew of divisions in the church at Corinth.	1 Corinthians 1:11
Claudia	Christian of Rome.	2 Timothy 4:21
Damaris	Woman of Athens converted under Paul's ministry.	Acts 17:34
Dorcas (Tabitha)	Christian in Joppa who was raised from the dead by Peter.	Acts 9:36-41
Drusilla	Wife of Felix, governor of Judea.	Acts 24:24
Elizabeth	Mother of John the Baptist.	Luke 15:13
Eunice	Mother of Timothy.	2 Timothy 1:5
Herodias	Queen who demanded the execution of John the Baptist.	Matthew 14:3-10
Joanna	Provided for the material needs of Jesus.	Luke 8:3
Lois	Grandmother of Timothy.	2 Timothy 1:5
Lydia	Converted under Paul's ministry in Philippi.	Acts 16:14
Martha and Mary	Sisters of Lazarus; friends of Jesus.	Luke 10:38-42
Mary Magdalene	Woman from whom Jesus cast out demons.	Matthew 27:56-61 Mark 16:9
Phoebe	A servant, some believe to be a deaconess, in the church at Cenchrea.	Romans 16:1-2
Priscilla	Wife of Aquila; laborer with Paul at Corinth and Ephesus.	Acts 18:2,18-19
Salome	Mother of the disciples James and John.	Matthew 20:20-24
Sapphira	Held back goods from the early Christian community.	Acts 5:1
Susanna	Provided for the material needs of Jesus.	Luke 8:3

APPLIED LEARNING PAGE
DISCIPLES AND RELIGIOUS SECTS

Which Disciple walked on Water to Jesus? _____

Which two Disciples are the sons of Zebedee? _____

Which Disciple betrayed Jesus? _____

Which Disciple denied Jesus? _____

Which Disciple was a Tax Collector? _____

Which of the 12 Disciples was the first killed? (Acts 12:2) _____

To bring the number back up to twelve after Judas betrayed Jesus, who was chosen by the remaining eleven apostles to be the 12th Disciple? _____

Which Disciple wanted to actually see and touch Jesus after His Resurrection before he would believe? _____

Look at page 133: Which religious sect was a religious and political group amongst the Jews who strictly observed the Jewish law? Focused on 'outward' forms of righteousness more than 'inward' and believed in the resurrection of the dead.

_____

Look at page 133: Which Religious Sect did not believe in the resurrection, angels, or spirits? They were enemies of Christ. _____

Look at page 133: Which Religious Sect was a mixed race, descendents of Jews and gentiles brought in by the Assyrian king during Israel's captivity? They were despised by the Jews.

_____

HOLY WEEK
EVENTS

DAY	EVENT	SCRIPTURE
Sunday	Jesus triumphal entry into Jerusalem.	Mark 11:1-11
Monday	Cleanses the temple in Jerusalem.	Mark 11:15-19
Tuesday	The Sanhedrin challenges Jesus' authority; Jesus foretells the destruction of Jerusalem and His return; Mary anoints Jesus at Bethany; Judas bargains with the Jewish rulers to betray Jesus for money.	Luke 20:1-8 Matthew 24:25 John 12:2-8 Luke 22:3-6
Wednesday	No recorded Bible events	
Thursday	Jesus eats the Passover meal with His disciples and institutes the Memorial Supper; Jesus prays in Gethsemane for His disciples.	John 13:1-30; Mark 14:22-26; John 17
Friday	Jesus betrayal and arrest in the Garden of Gethsemane; Jesus questioned by Annas, the former high priest; Condemned by Caiaphas and the Sanhedrin; Peter denies Jesus three times; Jesus is formally condemned by the Sanhedrin; Judas commits suicide; The trial of Jesus before Pilate; Jesus' appearance before Herod Antipas; Formally sentenced to death by Pilate; Jesus is mocked and crucified between two thieves; The veil of the temple is torn. His burial in the tomb of Joseph of Arimathea.	Mark 14:43-50 John 18:12-24 Mark 14:53-65 John 18:15-27 Luke 22:66-71 Matthew 27:3-10 Luke 23:1-5 Luke 23:6-12 Luke 23:13-25 Mark 15:16-27 Matthew 27:51-56 John 19:31-42
Sunday	Jesus is raised from the dead with all power and victory!	Luke 24:1-9

THE SEVEN LAST WORDS OF JESUS FROM THE CROSS

✝ Jesus arrived at Golgotha (Matthew 27:33; Mark 15:22; Luke 23:33; John 19:17).

✝ He refused the offer of vinegar to drink mixed with gall (Matthew 27:34; Mark 15:23).

✝ He was nailed to the cross between the two thieves (Matthew 27:35-38; Mark 15:24-28; Luke 23:33-38; John 19:18).

✝ He gave His first cry from the cross: **"Father, forgive them, for they know not what they do"** (Luke 23:34).

✝ The soldiers took Jesus' garments and cast lots (Matthew 27:35; Mark 15:24; Luke 23:34; John 19:23).

✝ The Jews mocked Jesus (Matthew 27:39-43; Mark 15:29-32; Luke 23:35-37).

✝ He conversed with the two thieves (Luke 23:39-43).

✝ He gave His second cry from the cross, **"Verily I say unto thee, to day shall thou be with me in paradise."** (Luke 23:43).

✝ He spoke the third time, "Jesus spoke to His mother Mary and His disciple John. **"Woman, behold thy son! Behold thy mother!"** (John 19:26-27).

✝ Darkness covered the earth from noon to 3 p.m. (Matthew 27:45; Mark 15:33; Luke 23:44).

✝ He gave His fourth cry, **"Eli, Eli, lama sabachthani?** That is to say, **My God, my God, why hast thou forsaken me?** (Matthew 27:46-47; Mark 15:34-36).

✝ His fifth cry was, **"I thirst**." (John 19:28).

✝ He drank vinegar from a sponge (Matthew 27:48; Mark 15:36, John 19:29).

✝ His gave His sixth cry, **"It is finished"** (John 19:30).

✝ He cried a seventh time, **"Father, into your hands I commend my spirit"** (Luke 23:46).

✝ He yielded up His spirit (Matthew 27:50; Mark 15:37; Luke 23:46; John 19:30).

✝ The sun was darkened and the temple curtain was torn in two (Matthew 27:51; Mark 15:38; Luke 23:45).

✝ Roman soldiers admitted, **"Truly he was the Son of God"** (Matthew 27:54; Mark 15:39).

FORTY DAYS
RESURRECTION TO ASCENSION

SUNDAY MORNING
✝ An angel rolled away the stone from Jesus' tomb before sunrise (Matthew 28:2-4).

✝ Women who followed Jesus visited Jesus' tomb and discovered He was missing (Matthew 28:1; Mark 16:1-4; Luke 24:1-3; John 20:1).

✝ Mary Magdalene left to tell Peter and John (John 20:1-2).

✝ The other women, remaining at the tomb, saw two angels who told them that Jesus had risen (Matthew 28:5-7; Mark 16:5-7; Luke 24:4-8).

✝ Peter and John visited Jesus' tomb (Luke 24:12; John 20:3-10).

✝ Mary Magdalene returned to the tomb and Jesus appeared to her alone in the garden (Mark 16:9-11; John 20:11-18) **His first appearance**.

✝ Jesus appeared to the other women (Mary, mother of James, Salome, and Joanna) (Matthew 28:8-10) **His second appearance**.

✝ Those who guarded Jesus' tomb reported to the religious rulers how the angel rolled away the stone. They were then bribed with money to lie. (Matthew 28:11-15).

✝ Jesus appeared to Peter (1 Corinthians 15:5) **His third appearance**.

SUNDAY AFTERNOON
✝ Jesus appeared to two men on the road to Emmaus (Mark 16:12-13; Luke 24:13-32) **His fourth appearance**.

SUNDAY EVENING
✝ The two disciples from Emmaus told others they saw Jesus (Luke 24:33-35).

✝ Jesus appeared to 10 apostles, Thomas was absent, in the Upper Room (Luke 24:36-43; John 20:19-25) **His fifth appearance**.

THE FOLLOWING SUNDAY
✝ Jesus appeared to the 11 Apostles, including Thomas and Thomas now believed (John 20:26-28) **His sixth appearance**.

THE FOLLOWING 32 DAYS
✝ Jesus appeared to seven disciples by the Sea of Galilee and performed a miracle of the fish (John 21:1-14) **His seventh appearance**.

✝ Jesus appeared to 500 (including the Eleven) at a mountain in Galilee (Matthew 28:16-20; Mark 16:15-18; 1 Corinthians 15:6) **His eighth appearance**.

✝ Jesus appeared to His half-brother James (1 Corinthians 15:7) **His ninth appearance**.

✝ At Jerusalem Jesus appeared again to His disciples (Luke 24:44-49; Acts 1:3-8) **His tenth appearance.**

✝ On the Mount of Olives **Jesus ascended into Heaven** while the disciples watched. (Mark 16:19-20; Luke 24:50-53; Acts 1:9-12).

HOLY COMMUNION

The Lord Jesus instituted Holy Communion on the night of His betrayal, while eating the Passover supper with His Disciples. Holy Communion is a sacrament like baptism and foot washing that the Lord commanded Believers to keep in expressing that Christ is our Lord. Jesus held a final supper with His disciples during the Passover feast in Jerusalem. The bread which He broke is to remind us of His body which had been broken for us. The wine is to remind us of His blood which was shed by the crown of thorns, the whipping of His flesh, the nails through His hands and feet, and the spear to His sides. Jesus told His Disciples that whenever they ate the bread and drank from the cup it was to remind them of what He had done.

> 1 Corinthians 11:24-25: The Lord Jesus the same night in which he was betrayed took bread: And when he had given thanks, he brake it, and said, take, eat: this is my body, which is broken for you: this do in remembrance of me. After the same manner also he took the cup, when he had supped, saying, this cup is the new testament in my blood: this do ye, as oft as ye drink it, in remembrance of me.

Believers shouldn't take Holy Communion haphazardly and on the other hand we shouldn't avoid or reject it. When we take Holy Communion we are openly expressing that Christ is our Lord. By receiving His spiritual flesh and blood, we openly express that Christ lives in us and we in Him.

> 1 Corinthians 11:27-29: Wherefore whosoever shall eat this bread, and drink this cup of the Lord, unworthily, shall be guilty of the body and blood of the Lord. But let a man examine himself, and so let him eat of that bread, and drink of that cup. For he that eateth and drinketh unworthily, eateth and drinketh damnation to himself, not discerning the Lord's body. For this cause many are weak and sickly among you, and many sleep.

> John 6:53-54: Verily, verily, I say unto you, except ye eat the flesh of the Son of man, and drink his blood; ye have no life in you. Whoso eateth my flesh, and drinketh my blood, hath eternal life; and I will raise him up at the last day.

It is important that we take Holy Communion seriously and solemnly knowing that we are partaking of Christ's body and blood. In clinical practice there are four main blood types: A, B, O, and AB. If you ever need a blood transfusion, you must receive the right blood type or your body will reject it. If the wrong blood is given, your immune system will recognize it. Your white blood cells will attack, destroy the new blood, and make you sick. In a spiritual since, before we take the Lord's Holy blood we must be Holy. If sin is in your life, ask for forgiveness so that you may partake of the Lord's Supper.

HISTORY 01 BOOK - ACTS

Acts, whose full title is "Acts of the Apostles," describes the adventures of the 11 apostles that remain after Jesus' resurrection. This book starts out with the apostles picking a twelfth "apostle" to replace Judas, who committed suicide after betraying Jesus. Acts is a crucial book in the Scripture in that it serves as the bridge between the Gospels and the Epistles. It narrates the continuing work of the resurrected Jesus through His church.

AUTHOR: Luke who was a physician

APPROXIMATE DATE: A.D. 63

THEME: History and Theology

MAJOR CONTENTS
1. The birth of the church through the ministry of Peter (2:1-12:25)
2. The spread of the Gospel in Jerusalem (2:1-8:4)
3. Ananias and Sapphira (5:1-11)
4. The spread of the Gospel in all Judea and Samaria (8:5-12:25)
5. The confirmation of new churches (15:36-41)
6. The ministry of Paul and Silas (16:1-18:22)
7. The third missionary journey (18:23-21:16)
8. Paul takes the Gospel to Rome (21:17-28:31)
9. Paul imprisoned at Caesarea for two years (24:1-27)
10. Paul speaks to Festus (25:1-12)
11. Paul speaks to Festus, Agrippa, and Bernice (25:13-26:32)
12. Paul sails for Rome and under house arrest for two years (27:1-28:31)

SCRIPTURE MEMORIZATION

Acts 1:8: But ye shall receive _____, after that the Holy Ghost is come upon you: and ye shall be _____ unto me both in Jerusalem, and in all Judaea, and in Samaria, and unto the uttermost part of the earth.

Acts 2:1: And when the day of _____ was fully come, they were all with one _____ in one place.

Acts 2:15-17: For these are not _____, as ye suppose, seeing it is but the third hour of the day. But this is that which was spoken by the prophet _____. And it shall come to pass in the _____ days, saith God, I will pour out of my Spirit upon all flesh: and your sons and your _____ shall prophesy, and your young men shall see visions, and your old men shall dream dreams.

Acts 2:38: Then Peter said unto them, _____, and be _____ every one of you in the name of _____ Christ for the remission of sins, and ye shall receive the gift of the _____ Ghost.

Acts 2:41: On the day of Pentecost, how many people were baptized? _____

Acts 5:34: What was the name of the Pharisee who was a doctor of the law?
_____

Acts 6:1-4: How many men did the brethren choose to take over the business of the church of serving tables and looking after the widows? _____

Acts 7:58-60: Which Disciple was stoned to death? _____

Acts 9:3-6: What road did Saul become a Christian on?_____

Acts 9:9: Who was made blind for three days? _____

Acts 9:37-42: Which Disciple raised Dorcas from the dead?_____

Acts 10:25-26: _____knelt to Peter and was told by Peter:
_____.

Acts 16:26: What opened the doors when Paul and Silas were in prison? _____

Acts 16:31: And they said, _____ on the Lord Jesus Christ, and thou shalt be saved, and thy _____.

Acts 18:2: What was Aquila's wife named? _____

Acts 20:9: This man went to sleep, fell out of the window, and was considered dead during one of Paul's long sermons. _____

Acts 26:28: Who was **"almost persuaded"** to believe in Jesus Christ based on the sermon of Paul? _____

THE GOSPEL AND HISTORY
COURSEWORK

HOMEWORK ASSIGNMENTS

QUESTIONS I HAVE FOR A BIBLE TEACHER

SECTION SPECIAL NOTES

PAULINE EPISTLES
13 BOOKS

ROMANS

1 CORINTHIANS

2 CORINTHIANS

GALATIANS

EPHESIANS

PHILIPPIANS

COLOSSIANS

1 THESSALONIANS

2 THESSALONIANS

1 TIMOTHY   **PASTORAL EPISTLES**

2 TIMOTHY   **PASTORAL EPISTLES**

TITUS   **PASTORAL EPISTLES**

PHILEMON

NOTE: 1-2 Timothy and Titus are called "pastoral epistles" because they discuss mainly the duties for pastors and spiritual leaders.

ROMANS

The book of Romans describes why a person would want to be a Christian, and how they can become one. The way of a sinner's acceptance with God, or justification in his sight, merely by grace, through faith in the righteousness of Christ is plainly stated. It is recommended to read Mark, Acts and then Romans to get a good foundation of Jesus Christ and the plan of Salvation.

AUTHOR: Paul

APPROXIMATE DATE: A.D. 57

THEME: The Doctrine of Salvation

MAJOR CONTENTS
1. The universal state of condemnation (1:18-3:20)
2. The determined degradation of the race (1:18-32)
3. Inexcusable of the race (2:1-13)
4. Gentile guilt through conscience (2:14-16)
5. Jewish guilt through the Law (2:17-29)
6. The inability of the law to bring justification (3:1-20)
7. God's provision through justification (3:21-5:21)
8. God's provision through sanctification (6:1-8:39)
9. God's provision for Israel (9:1-11:36)
10. The ethics of God's people (12:1-15:16)
11. Concluding personal matters (15:17-16:16)

NOTE: The book of Romans is often referred to as the Roman's road of salvation.

THE ROMAN'S ROAD
PLAN OF SALVATION

Rom 3:23: For all have _____, and come short of the _____ of God.

Rom 5:1: Therefore being _____by faith, we have _____ with God through our Lord Jesus Christ.

Rom 5:8: But God _____his love toward us, in that, while we were yet sinners, Christ _____for us.

Rom 6:23: For the wages of _____ is death; but the gift of God is eternal life through Jesus Christ our Lord.

Rom 8:28: And we _____ that all things work together for _____to them that love God, to them who are the called according to his _____.

Rom 10:9: That if thou shalt _____with thy mouth the Lord Jesus, and shalt _____in thine heart that God hath raised him from the dead, thou shalt be _____.

Rom 12:1-2: I beseech you therefore, brethren, by the mercies of God, that ye present your _____ a living sacrifice, holy, acceptable unto God, which is your reasonable service. And be not _____to this world: but be ye _____ by the renewing of your mind, that ye may prove what is that good, and acceptable, and _____, will of God.

Rom 12:21: Be not overcome of _____, but overcome evil with _____.

Rom 14:16: Let not then your _____be evil spoken of.

1 CORINTHIANS

First Corinthians is a letter written to the most corrupt Christian church addressed in the Bible. The peace of this church was disturbed by false teachers. This epistle was written to rebuke disorderly conduct.

AUTHOR: Paul

APPROXIMATE DATE: A.D. 56-57

THEME: Overcoming Problems in the Church

MAJOR CONTENTS
1. Disorders reported to Paul (1:10-6:20)
2. Division at Corinth (1:10-4:21)
3. Church discipline (5:1-13)
4. Judicial entanglements (6:1-8)
5. Immorality (6:9-20)
6. Problems raised by the Corinthians (7:1-10:33)
7. Marriage (7:1-40)
8. Meat offered to Idols (8:1-10:33)
9. More disorders reported to Paul (11:1-15:58)
10. Corinth women's position and covering (11:1-16)
11. The Lord's Supper (11:17-34)
12. Spiritual gifts (12:1-14:40)
13. Resurrection (15:1-58)
14. The offering (16:1-9)

SCRIPTURE MEMORIZATION

1 Cor 1:10: Now I beseech you, _____, by the name of our Lord Jesus Christ, that ye all _____ the same thing, and that there be no divisions among you; but that ye be perfectly joined together in the same mind and in the same judgment.

1 Cor 3:6: I have _____, Apollos _____but God gave the increase.

1 Cor 12:26: And whether one member _____, all the members suffer with it; or one member be honored, all the members _____ with it.

2 CORINTHIANS

Second Corinthians can be thought of as the continuation to 1 Corinthians. The church followed some of the earlier advice, but still had some problems. A special feature of this book is that it lets Christians know what their heavenly bodies will be like.

AUTHOR: Paul

APPROXIMATE DATE: A.D. 56-57

THEME: Defense of Paul's Apostleship: The church at Corinth had been invaded by false teachers. Eloquent in speech, with a charming and impressive manner, these intruders were calling into question Paul's apostolic credentials.

MAJOR CONTENTS

1. Paul explains his ministry of reconciliation (1:12-7:16)
2. Paul defends his integrity (1:12-2:4)
3. Paul urges the church to forgive the "Offender" (2:5-11)
4. Paul describes his Apostolic ministry (2:12-6:10)
5. Paul exhorts the readers to stay away from sin (6:11-7:1)
6. Believers to make room for Him in their hearts (7:2-4)
7. The report of Titus is an encouragement to Paul (7:5-16)
8. Paul encourages Grace giving and the collection for Judea (8:1-9:15)
9. Paul encourages them by the example of the Macedonians (8:1-7)
10. Paul reminds them of the example of the Lord Jesus Christ (8:8-9)
11. Paul gives instruction in how to help the Saints (8:10-9:5)
12. The blessings which will come through Grace giving (9:6-15)
13. Paul defends His apostolic authority (10:1-13:10)
14. His call to the ministry is from the Lord (10:1-18)
15. His Apostleship is authenticated by God (11:1-12:13)
16. Restore discipline and order at Corinth (12:14-13:10)

SCRIPTURE MEMORIZATION

2 Cor 6:14: Be ye not _____ yoked together with unbelievers: for what fellowship hath righteousness with unrighteousness? And what _____hath light with darkness?

2 Cor 11:25: How many times was Paul beaten with rods but continued to preach about Jesus? _____

SPIRITUAL GIFTS

Apostle

Teacher

Working of Miracles

Word of Wisdom

Evangelists

Gift of Faith

Gift of Tongues

Ministry-Serving

Rulers

Gift of Mercy

Prophet

Pastor

Discernment of Spirits

Word of Knowledge

Exhortation-Encouragement

Gift of Healing

Interpretation of Tongues

Gift of Administration

Gift of Helps

Gift of Giving

Romans 12:4-8

1 Corinthians 12: 1-12

Ephesians 4:11-12

GALATIANS

The letter to the Galatians addresses a problem seen in many churches today: adding man-made requirements for being a Christian. This book reveals how free from external requirements Christianity really is. This is another good book to learn what separates true Christianity from cults that masquerade themselves as a "superior" Christianity.

AUTHOR: Paul

APPROXIMATE DATE: Galatians may have been written in A.D. 48-49, after the first missionary journey and just prior to the Conference. Others date the letter A.D. 55-57, several years after the Jerusalem conference.

THEME: The epistle is a heated, vigorous, uncompromising defense of (1) Paul's own authority as an apostle of Jesus Christ, and (2) the gospel of the grace of God.

MAJOR CONTENTS
1. Paul's independence of human authority (1:10-2:21)
2. Paul's Gospel received directly from God (1:10-12)
3. Evidence substantiating the proposition (1:13-2:21)
4. The failure of legalism (3:1-4:31)
5. The personal experience of the Galatians (3:1-5)
6. The example of Abraham (3:6-9)
7. The curse of the Law (3:10-14)
8. The priority of promise (3:15-18)
9. The purpose of the Law (3:19-4:7)
10. The danger of returning to bondage (4:8-11)
11. A contrast between the motives of Paul and the legalists (4:12-20)
12. An Old Testament illustration of Law versus promise (4:21-31)
13. The practical argument: Liberty in Christ (5:1-6:10)
14. Liberty excluding Circumcision (5:1-6)
15. Liberty as opposed by Legalists (5:7-12)
16. Liberty defined (5:13-15)
17. Liberty and the Spirit filled life (5:16-26)
18. Fruits of the Spirit (5:22-23)
19. Liberty and responsibility for the burdened (6:1-5)
20. Liberty and the responsibility to do good (6:6-10)

GALATIANS

SCRIPTURE MEMORIZATION

Gal 1:13: Was Paul, before his conversion, a persecutor of Christians? _____

Gal 3:28: There is neither Jew nor _____, there is neither bond nor free, there is neither _____ nor _____ for ye are all one in Christ Jesus.

Gal 5:1: Stand fast therefore in the _____ wherewith Christ hath made us free, and be not _____ again with the yoke of _____.

Gal 5:7: Ye did run _____; who did _____ you that ye should not obey the truth?

Gal 5:16: This I say then, _____ in the Spirit, and ye shall not _____ the lust of the flesh.

GAL 5:22-23: THE FRUIT OF THE SPIRIT

LOVE, JOY, PEACE, LONGSUFFERING, GENTLENESS, GOODNESS, FAITH, MEEKNESS, TEMPERANCE.

EPHESIANS

Ephesians has at least three special points of interest. First, it explains how people receive special abilities when they become Christians. Second, it outlines the roles of the husband, wife, and child in the family. Third, it describes the "spiritual battle" taking place around us.

AUTHOR: Paul

APPROXIMATE DATE: As one of Paul's "Prison Epistles", the letter would be dated A.D. 60-63, corresponding to the time of his first Roman imprisonment.

THEME: Unity in Christ

MAJOR CONTENTS
1. God's Sovereign choice of Believers (1:3-6)
2. The wisdom of God in providing redemption through Christ (1:7-10)
3. The Holy Spirit for the inheritance of the Saints (1:11-14)
4. Thanksgiving and prayer for his readers (1:15-23)
5. Thanksgiving for faith and love (1:15-16)
6. Prayer for wisdom (1:17-23)
7. Doctrinal section (2:1-3:21)
8. The greatness of Christian salvation (2:1-3:13)
9. Prayer for inward Spiritual strength (3:14-21)
10. Practical section (4:1-6:20)
11. The problem of unity (4:1-16)
12. The old life and the new (4:17-5:21)
13. The Christian home (5:22-6:9)
14. The Christian warfare (6:10-20)

SCRIPTURE MEMORIZATION

Ephesians 4:4-5: There is one body, and one Spirit, even as ye are called in one hope of your calling; one _____, one _____, one _____.

Ephesians 6:13-18:

The Breastplate of _____

The Helmet of _____

The Shield of _____

The Sword of _____

THE SEARCH FOR GOD'S ARMOR

God tells us to put on the full armor of God, so that when the day of evil comes, we may be able to stand. Use this Word Search to familiarize yourself with the different pieces of God's armor.

```
Q S H Q A J W V Y G L S S V I
E X A D L E I H S P H S M T G
I V D L B T G L K D E N I X P
Q P N R V X R Y O N L P D I L
S H O E S A F U S V M B X X I
H J J R E E T U R E E X J K
W X U S I P O I W H T L M G J
Y G H O A E N H O L W T O P D
E V K C T F E K M N L S R N H
E P Q H B R E A S T P L A T E
J C G Z H D C Q I I L F F H V
D I A T G R T C R Z G O L V I
R R I E F O L I U O Z Z S F V
A A A H P W T Z U O L N R S X
F P A X P S T F V A J S G W Q
```

WORDS MAY BE ACROSS, DOWN OR DIAGONAL

BELT
SALVATION
BREASTPLATE
SHIELD
RIGHTEOUSNESS
SHOES
HELMET
SPIRIT
PEACE
SWORD
FAITH
TRUTH

PHILIPPIANS

Philippians is a wonderful book to help you with dealing with everyday stress. The Philippians felt a very deep interest for the apostle. The scope of the epistle is to confirm them in the faith, to encourage them to walk in the ways of Christ, to caution them against judaizing teachers, and to express gratitude for their Christian bounty.

AUTHOR: Paul

APPROXIMATE DATE: Philippians was probably written while Paul was first imprisoned in Rome A.D. 60-63.

THEME: Rejoice in the Lord: The theme of the book of Philippians is "rejoicing in the Lord." The keynote is joy. Paul's immediate purpose is to assure the Philippian church of his appreciation for their lives and for the kindness demonstrated in their recent gifts.

MAJOR CONTENTS
1. Paul's thanksgiving and prayer for the Philippians (1:3-11)
2. Paul's situation in Rome (1:12-26)
3. Imprisonment and opposition (1:12-18)
4. Expectation of deliverance (1:19-26)
5. Paul's exhortations (1:27-2:4)
6. Steadfastness (1:27-30)
7. Meekness and unity (2:1-4)
8. Paul's great example (2:5-18)
9. The exaltation of Christ (2:9-11)
10. The working out of salvation (2:12-18)
11. Paul's messengers to the Church (2:19-30)
12. Paul's warning against heresies (3:1-4:1)
13. Paul's appreciation for the Philippians' gifts (4:10-20)

PHILIPPIANS

SCRIPTURE MEMORIZATION

Phil 2:10: That at the name of Jesus every _____ should bow, of things in _____, and things in _____, and things under the earth.

Phil 2:11: And that every _____ should confess that Jesus Christ is Lord, to the glory of God the Father.

Phil 4:7: And the _____ of God, which passeth all understanding, shall _____your _____and _____ through Christ Jesus.

Phil 4:13: I can do _____ things through Christ which _____ me.

COLOSSIANS

Colossians is another short book. It is especially suited to reading by new Christians. This epistle was sent because of some difficulties which arose among the Colossians, probably from false teachers. The scope of the epistle is to show, that all hope of man's redemption is founded on Christ. The Colossians are cautioned against the devices of judaizing teachers, and also against the notions of carnal wisdom, and human inventions and traditions, as not consistent with full reliance on Christ. In the first two chapters the apostle tells them what they must believe, and in the two last what they must do; the doctrine of faith, and the precepts of life for salvation.

AUTHOR: The Epistle to the Colossians is one of the four "Prison Epistles" It was written by the apostle **Paul** (1:1) while he was a prisoner in Rome awaiting trial (4:3, 10, 18).

APPROXIMATE DATE: The most acceptable date for this epistle is A.D. 60-63. It was written about the same time as the letters to Philemon and Ephesus, and it has much in common with both epistles.

THEME: Combating False Teachings: The Epistle to the Colossians is written to combat an unspecified but dangerous error that crept into the church some six years after its founding. Thus Paul writes to combat certain false teachings about Christ and to give encouragement for the Christian life.

MAJOR CONTENTS
1. Prayer for the Colossians (1:3-14)
2. Paul's doctrine of the person of Christ (1:15-23)
3. Paul's part in God's plan (1:24-2:5)
4. Paul's warning against false teachings (2:6-15)
5. Paul's exposure of threatening heresy (2:16-3:4)
6. New Man in Christ (3:5-17)
7. Practical instructions (3:18-4:6)
8. Paul's commendation and closing salutations (4:7-17)

SCRIPTURE MEMORIZATION
Col 2:21: Touch not; _____not; handle not.

Col 3:16: Let the word of Christ dwell in you _____ in all

_____; teaching and admonishing one another in psalms and

_____and spiritual songs, singing with grace in your hearts to the Lord.

1 THESSALONIANS

First Thessalonians contains one of the best descriptions in the Bible of what happens to departed Christians. This epistle is generally considered to have been the first of those written by Paul. The occasion seems to have been the good report of the steadfastness of the church at Thessalonica in the faith of the Gospel.

AUTHOR: Paul

APPROXIMATE DATE: A.D.51-52

THEME: Every chapter of the epistle contains some positive reference to the promised return of Christ and its significance to believers.

MAJOR CONTENTS
1. Personal testimony (1:1-3:13)
2. A practical appeal (4:1-5:22)

SCRIPTURE MEMORIZATION

1 Th 4:7: For God hath not called us unto _____, but unto _____.

1 Th 4:11: And that ye study to be_____ and to do your own _____, and to work with your own hands, as we commanded you.

1 Th 5:17: _____without ceasing.

1 Th 5:19: Quench not the _____.

1 Th 5:22: Abstain from all _____ of evil.

2 THESSALONIANS

Second Thessalonians is a short "sequel" to 1 Thessalonians. The second epistle to the Thessalonians was written soon after the first. The apostle was told that, from some expressions in his first letter, many expected the second coming of Christ was at hand, and that the Day of Judgment would arrive in their time. Some of these neglected their worldly duties. Paul wrote again to correct their error, which hindered the spread of the Gospel. He had written agreeably to the words of the prophets of the Old Testament; and he tells them there were many counsels of the Most High yet to be fulfilled, before that day of the Lord should come, though, because it is sure, he had spoken of it as near. The subject led to a remarkable foretelling, of some of the future events which were to take place in the after-ages of the Christian church, and which show the prophetic spirit the apostle possessed.

AUTHOR: Paul

APPROXIMATE DATE: A.D.51-52: A few months after writing 1 Thessalonians in A.D. 51-52, Paul writes a second letter under very similar circumstances. He is still in Corinth and is eager to communicate with the believers in Thessalonica.

THEME: Understanding the Christian Life. The immediate cause for this second letter to the Thessalonians was evidently a spurious letter incorrectly attributed to Paul which had caused confusion concerning the order of events upon the return of Christ.

MAJOR CONTENTS
1. The privilege of prayer (1:3-12)
2. A time for thanksgiving (1:3)
3. A foundation for praise (1:4)
4. A coming judgment (1:5-10)
5. A personal petition (1:11-12)
6. The promise of His return (2:1-17)
7. A word of clarification concerning the day of the Lord (2:1-2)
8. A word of description about the man of sin (2:3-12)
9. A word of exhortation to Believers (2:13-17)
10. The practice of Godliness (3:1-15)
11. Holiness and the word of the Lord (3:1-2)
12. Faithfulness to the Lord (3:3-5)
13. The people of the Lord (3:6-15)

SCRIPTURE MEMORIZATION
Select two of your own scriptures from this book to memorize and recite.

THE CHRISTIAN LIFE

Authors Unknown
Copied from Internet public domain

CHRISTIANS	TEXT	MEANING
SOLDIERS	2 Tim. 2:3-4	Like a single-minded soldier, we should respond to the orders of our commanding officer, the Lord Jesus Christ.
FARMERS	2 Tim. 2:6	Farmers labor strenuously and consistently in order to reap a fruitful harvest. We must work hard in serving the Lord.
ATHLETES	2 Tim. 2:5	Athletes follow strict training rules so as to avoid being disqualified from their race; we must stay in the Christian race following the rules of the Bible.
WORKERS	2 Tim. 2:15	Our work is to "rightly divide" or correctly handle God's Word so as to avoid embarrassment.
VESSELS	2 Tim. 2:20-21	We must keep ourselves pure, like a clean dish, so that we will be "useful for the Master."
FISHERS OF MEN	Matt. 4:19	As fishermen, we are called to "catch" men with the Good News of Christ.
SALT	Matt. 5:13	As salt, we act as a Godly preservative in an evil society; moreover, we make people thirsty to know the Lord.
LIGHT	Matt. 5:14-16	As light, we point the way to reconciliation with God, and we reflect God's character, for He is the Light (John 1:7).
BRANCHES	John 15:5	As branches, we bear Godly fruit as long as we are attached to Christ who is the True Vine.
STEWARDS	1 Cor. 4:1-2	Like administrators, we have responsibilities to manage. God will evaluate how we handle the resources He has given us.
AMBASSADORS	2 Cor. 5:20	We are representatives of God's kingdom to the lost citizens of this world.
LIVING STONES	1 Pet. 2:5	In former days, God dwelt in a physical temple; now He dwells in His people, the church.
PRIESTS	1 Pet. 2:5-10	Like priests, we have the privilege of approaching near to God, and the responsibility of helping others in reconciling themselves to Him.
SOJOURNERS	1 Pet. 2:11	As children of God, we do not belong to the world. This world is not our home; we are only "passing through."

1 TIMOTHY

If you want to learn what separates a real church leader from a phony, go to First Timothy. The design of the epistle appears to be, that Timothy having been left at Ephesus, Paul wrote to instruct him in the choice of proper officers in the church, as well as in the exercise of a regular ministry. Also, to caution against the influence of false teachers, who by subtle distinctions and endless disputes, corrupted the purity and simplicity of the gospel. He presses upon him constant regard to the greatest diligence, faithfulness, and zeal. These subjects occupy the first four chapters; the fifth chapter instructs respecting particular classes; in the latter part, controversies and disputes are condemned, the love of money blamed, and the rich exhorted to good works. First and Second Timothy and Titus are commonly designated the Pastoral Epistles because they provide instruction and guidance concerning the care and protection of the churches. The three letters focus upon church life as well as upon leadership qualifications and responsibilities. The need for sound doctrine and a life of godliness are recurring themes throughout these last three letters written by Paul.

AUTHOR: Paul

APPROXIMATE DATE: A.D. 62-66

THEME: Dealing with false doctrine. Determining true and false ministry

MAJOR CONTENTS
1. True and false ministry (1:3-20)
2. Instructions for Christian worship (2:1-15)
3. Prayer and the mediator (2:1-8)
4. Women and modesty (2:9-15)
5. The qualifications of Bishops and Deacons (3:1-13)
6. The office of a Bishop (3:1-7)
7. The office of a Deacon (3:8-13)
8. The reason for writing (3:14-16)
9. Error and its correction (4:1-16)
10. The charge of a good ministry (4:6-16)
11. The treatment of Widows, Elders, and others (5:1-6:2)
12. The false teacher contrasted with the true teacher (6:3-21)

1 TIMOTHY

SCRIPTURE MEMORIZATION

1 Tim 3:16:   And without _____ great is the _____ of godliness:
God was _____ in the flesh, justified in the Spirit, seen of angels, preached
unto the Gentiles, _____on in the world, received up into glory.

1 Tim 6:7: For we brought nothing into this _____, and it is certain we
can carry nothing out.

1 Tim 6:10: What is the root of all evil? _____

1 Tim 6:12: Fight the good _____ of faith, lay hold on eternal life, whereunto
thou art also called, and hast professed a good _____ before many witnesses.

2 TIMOTHY

The first design of this epistle seems to have been, to inform Timothy of what had occurred during the imprisonment of the apostle, and to request him to come to Rome. But being uncertain whether he should be suffered to live to see him, Paul gives a variety of advices and encouragements, for the faithful discharge of his ministerial duties. As this was a private epistle written to Paul's most intimate friend, under the miseries of imprisonment, and in the near prospect of death, it shows the temper and character of the apostle, and contains convincing proofs that he sincerely believed the doctrines he preached.

AUTHOR: Paul

APPROXIMATE DATE: A.D. 66-67

THEME: Steadfast Christian Living

MAJOR CONTENTS
1. Encouragement to faithful ministry (1:6-4:5)
2. Strength even during persecution (1:6-2:7)
3. False teaching (2:8-3:9)
4. Paul's example to follow (3:10-17)
5. Final exhortation (4:1-5)
6. Paul's situation (4:6-18)
7. Paul's final greetings (4:19-21)

SCRIPTURE MEMORIZATION

2 Tim 1:7: For God hath not given us the _____ of _____; but of power, and of _____, and of a sound _____.

2 Tim 2:15: Study to show thyself _____ unto God, a workman that needeth not to be _____, rightly dividing the word of truth.

2 Tim 3:5: Having a form of _____, but denying the _____ thereof: from such turn away.

2 Tim 4:2: Preach the word; be _____ in season, out of season; reprove, rebuke, _____ with all longsuffering and doctrine.

TITUS

Titus is a short letter of guidance and encouragement to a young pastor that includes great advice usable by all of us. This epistle mainly contains directions to Titus concerning the elders of the Church, and the manner in which he should give instruction; and the latter part tells him to urge obedience to magistrates, to enforce good works, avoid foolish questions, and shun heresies. The instructions the apostle gave are all plain and simple. The Christian religion was not formed to answer worldly or selfish views, but it is the wisdom of God and the power of God.

AUTHOR: Paul

APPROXIMATE DATE: A.D. 62-66: The epistle was evidently written during the same general period of time in which 1 Timothy was written, in the period which elapsed between Paul's first and second Roman imprisonments.

THEME: The theme of Titus is the proper relationship of God, the brethren, and society in general within the church.

MAJOR CONTENTS
1. Qualifications and responsibilities of Pastors (1:5-9)
2. The nature of heresy (1:10-16)
3. Community Christian ethics (2:1-3:2)
4. Instruction for Christian behavior (2:1-10)
5. Promise of Christ (2:11-3:2)
6. The nature of regeneration (3:3-7)
7. Final warnings(3:8-15)

SCRIPTURE MEMORIZATION

Titus 3:9: But avoid _____questions, and genealogies, and

_____, and strivings about the law; for they are unprofitable and vain.

PHILEMON

Philemon is a letter, a story, and a lesson rolled into one. Philemon was an inhabitant of Colosse, a person of some note and wealth, and a convert under the ministry of Paul. Onesimus was the slave of Philemon: having run away from his master, he went to Rome, where he was converted to the Christian faith, by the word as set forth by Paul, who kept him till his conduct proved the truth and sincerity of his conversion. He wished to repair the injury he had done to his master, but fearing the punishment his offence deserved might be inflicted, he entreated the apostle to write to Philemon. Paul seems no where to reason more beautifully, or to entreat more forcibly, than in this epistle.

AUTHOR: Paul

APPROXIMATE DATE: A.D. 60-63

THEME: Restoration of a Slave Brother: Paul's letter to Philemon on behalf of Onesimus reveals the transforming power of salvation in Jesus Christ. First, Onesimus himself was a runaway slave who had robbed his master Philemon and fled to Rome. Onesimus not only had been transformed on the inside, but also in Christ his relationship to Philemon had been lifted from that of a slave to that of "a beloved brother."

MAJOR CONTENTS
1. Paul's praise for Philemon (v. 4-7)
2. Paul's plea for Onesimus (v. 8-16)
3. Paul's pledge and assurance (v. 17-22)

SCRIPTURE MEMORIZATION

Philemon 1:3: Grace to you, and _____, from God our Father and the Lord Jesus Christ.

APPLIED LEARNING PAGE

WRITE THE NT GOSPEL AND FIRST HISTORY BOOK	WRITE THE NT PAULINE EPISTLES

PAULINE EPISTLES
13 BOOKS

APPLIED LEARNING PAGE

WHAT IS THE MISSING BOOK? _____

Romans
1 Corinthians
2 Corinthians
Galatians
Ephesians
Philippians
Colossians
1 Thessalonians
2 Thessalonians
1 Timothy
2 Timothy
Philemon

NOTE: All 13 Pauline Epistles (Letters) were written by the Apostle Paul.

APPLICATION
Write a sentence or song using the first letters of each book to help you memorize the 13 Pauline Epistles.

FUN LEARNING
Apply one of the fun learning techniques from the learning techniques page.

PAULINE EPISTLES
COURSEWORK

HOMEWORK ASSIGNMENTS

QUESTIONS I HAVE FOR A BIBLE TEACHER

SECTION SPECIAL NOTES

FIND THE MISSING BOOKS
WORKSHEET

WHAT ARE THE (2) TWO MISSING BOOKS?

_____

_____

Matthew
Mark
Luke
John
Acts
Romans
1 Corinthians
2 Corinthians
Ephesians
Philippians
Colossians
1 Thessalonians
2 Thessalonians
1 Timothy
2 Timothy
Philemon

GENERAL EPISTLES
08 BOOKS

HEBREWS

JAMES

1 PETER

2 PETER

1 JOHN

2 JOHN

3 JOHN

JUDE

HEBREWS

Hebrews is another of the most important books in the Bible. This epistle shows Christ as the end, foundation, body, and truth of the figures of the law, which of themselves were no virtue for the soul. The great truth set forth in this epistle is that Jesus of Nazareth is the true God. The unconverted Jews used many arguments to draw their converted brethren from the Christian faith. They represented the Law of Moses as superior to the Christian dispensation, and spoke against every thing connected with the Savior. The apostle, therefore, shows the superiority of Jesus of Nazareth, as the Son of God, and the benefits from his sufferings and death as the sacrifice for sin, so that the Christian religion is much more excellent and perfect than that of Moses. And the principal design seems to be, to bring the converted Hebrews forward in the knowledge of the gospel, and thus to establish them in the Christian faith, and to prevent their turning from it, against which they are earnestly warned. But while it contains many things suitable to the Hebrews of early times, it also contains many which can never cease to interest the church of God; for the knowledge of Jesus Christ is the very marrow and kernel of all the Scriptures. The ceremonial law is full of Christ, and all the gospel is full of Christ; the blessed lines of both Testaments meet in Him; and how they both agree and sweetly unite in Jesus Christ, is the chief object of the epistle to the Hebrews to discover.

AUTHOR: Unknown

APPROXIMATE DATE: A.D. 65

THEME: Jesus the Great High Priest: Hebrews sustains one thought from beginning to end: Jesus the High Priest, in His ministry and atonement for sins, is superior to anything offered by the collective ministry within Judaism. Only this book calls Jesus "High Priest."

MAJOR CONTENTS
1. The superiority of Christ, the revealer of God (1:5-7:28)
2. Superiority to angels as revealers of God (1:5-14)
3. Warning against neglect of Christ's revelation (2:1-4)
4. Revelation through perfect humanity (2:5-18)
5. Superiority to Moses as revealer of God (3:1-6)
6. Warning against becoming hardened (3:7-4:16)
7. Superiority to Aaron as revealer of God (5:1-10)
8. Warning against falling away (5:11-6:20)
9. The example of Melchizedek (7:1-28)
10. The better covenant of Christ's revelation (8:1-18)
11. Christ as High Priest (8:1-7)
12. The promise of the new covenant (8:8-13)
13. A prophecy in the old covenant (9:1-10)
14. An eternal Inheritance (9:11-14)

15. Sealing by Christ's sacrifice (9:15-22)
16. Ministering in the very presence of God (9:23-28)
17. Full and final provision for man's needs (10:1-18)
18. Faith related to Christ's revelation (10:19-11:40)
19. The necessity of Faith (10:19-25)
20. Warning concerning sinning willfully (10:26-31)
21. Genuine faith and perseverance (10:32-39)
22. The foundation of every experience with God (11:1-3)
23. The character of God's servants (11:4-38)
24. Vindication by Christ himself (11:39-40)
25. Living as a Reflection of Christ's Revelation (12:1-13:17)
26. Running the race of life (12:1-3)
27. God's discipline of His children (12:4-11)
28. Walking a straight path (12:12-17)
29. Warning against refusing Christ's demands (12:18-29)
30. Ethical demands (13:1-6)
31. Worthy examples to follow (13:7-8)
32. Life as worship (13:9-16)
33. The design of Spiritual authority (13:17)
34. A request for Prayer (13:18-19)
35. Personal greetings and observations (13:22-24)

SCRIPTURE MEMORIZATION

Heb 4:12: For the word of God is _____, and _____, and
sharper than any two edged _____, piercing even to the dividing asunder of
soul and spirit, and of the joints and marrow, and is a _____ of the thoughts and
intents of the heart.

Heb 6:12: That ye be not _____, but followers of them who through
_____ and _____ inherit the promises.

Heb 10:26: For if we sin _____ after that we have received the knowledge of
the _____, there remaineth no _____ sacrifice for sins.

Heb 11:1: Now faith is the substance of things _____ for, the
_____ of things not seen.

185

JAMES

James is a book written by the (half) brother of Jesus. You will find this book very relevant to today's world.

AUTHOR: James

APPROXIMATE DATE: A.D. 48-50

THEME: Practical Religion: The central theme of the epistle is practical, realistic religion which manifests itself in the behavior or the "works" of those who profess to have faith.

MAJOR CONTENTS

1. Genuine religion (1:2-27)
2. Illustrated by patience in trials and temptation (1:2-18)
3. Illustrated by Godly conduct (1:19-27)
4. Genuine faith (2:1-26)
5. Illustrated by impartiality (2:1-13)
6. Illustrated by works (2:14-26)
7. Genuine wisdom (3:1-18)
8. Illustrated by words (3:1-12)
9. Contrasted with false wisdom (3:13-18)
10. Genuine humility (4:1-5:6)
11. Worldly attitudes condemned (4:1-10)
12. Worldly actions condemned (4:11-5:6)
13. Genuine behavior awaiting the Lord's return (5:7-20)
14. Illustrated by patience (5:7-12)
15. Illustrated by prayer in Faith (5:13-18)
16. Illustrated by brotherly concern (5:19-20)

JAMES

SCRIPTURE MEMORIZATION

James 1:6: But let him ask in _____, nothing wavering. For he that
_____ is like a wave of the sea driven with the wind and tossed.

James 2:1-11: Is showing favoritism a sin? _____

James 2:17: Even so _____, if it hath not _____, is dead, being alone.

James 4:7: _____ yourselves therefore to God. _____ the
devil, and he will flee from you.

James 4:8: Draw nigh to God, and he will draw nigh to you. _____ your hands,
ye sinners; and purify your hearts, ye double minded.

James 4:10: _____ yourselves in the sight of the _____, and he shall
lift you up.

James 4:17: Therefore to him that _____ to do good, and doeth it not, to him it is
_____.

James 5:12: Should Christians swear? _____

James 5:20: Let him know, that he which _____ the sinner from the error of
his _____ shall save a soul from death, and shall hide a multitude of sins.

1 PETER

Would you like to hear from someone who literally walked the Earth with Jesus for three years? If so, this is a great book to read. The same great doctrines, as in Paul's epistles, are here applied to same practical purposes. And this epistle is remarkable for the sweetness, gentleness, and humble love, with which it is written. It gives a short, and yet a very clear summary, both of the consolations and the instructions needful for the encouragement and direction of a Christian in his journey to heaven, raising his thoughts and desires to that happiness, and strengthening him against all opposition in the way, both from corruption within, and temptations and afflictions without.

AUTHOR: Peter, the brother of Andrew and son of Jonah (Matt. 16:17), a fisherman of Bethsaida on the Sea of Galilee, is the author of both epistles which bear his name.

APPROXIMATE DATE: The approximate date for the writing of 1 Peter would then be A.D. 63 or 64, during the reign of Nero, under whose hand Peter eventually suffered martyrdom as Jesus had prophesied.

THEME: Encouragement in Suffering

MAJOR CONTENTS
1. Christ and the trial of faith (1:3-25)
2. The inheritance of faith (1:3-12)
3. The response of faith (1:13-17)
4. The birth of faith (1:18-25)
5. Christ and the life of faith (2:1-25)
6. The relationship of faith (2:1-10)
7. The walk of faith (2:11-19)
8. The example of faith (2:20-25)
9. Christ and the obedience of faith (3:1-22)
10. The house of faith (3:1-7)
11. The activity of faith (3:8-17)
12. The patience of faith (3:18-22)
13. Christ and the ethics of faith (4:1-19)
14. The reversals of faith (4:1-6)
15. The consummation of faith (4:7-14)
16. The posture of faith (4:15-19)
17. Christ and the Church of faith (5:1-9)
18. The victory of faith (5:5-9)

1 PETER

SCRIPTURE MEMORIZATION

1 Pet 1:7: That the _____ of your faith, being much more precious than of

_____ that perisheth, though it be tried with _____, might be found unto

praise and honor and glory at the appearing of Jesus Christ.

1 Pet 2:9: But ye are a _____ generation, a royal priesthood, an holy

_____, a peculiar people; that ye should show forth the

_____ of him who hath called you out of _____ into his

marvelous light.

1 Pet 4:18: And if the _____scarcely be saved, where shall the

ungodly and the sinner appear?

1 Pet 5:7: Casting all your _____ upon him; for he _____ for you.

2 PETER

This epistle clearly is connected with the former epistle of Peter. The apostle having stated the blessings, to which God has called Christians, exhorts those who had received these precious gifts, to endeavor to improve in graces and virtues. They are urged to this from the wickedness of false teachers. They are guarded against impostors and scoffers, by disproving their false assertions, and by showing why the great day of Christ's coming was delayed, with a description of its awful circumstances and consequences; and suitable exhortations to diligence and holiness are given.

AUTHOR: Peter

APPROXIMATE DATE: The second epistle was written shortly after the first, probably from the same location. Proper assignment is then A.D. 65-66.

THEME: A variety of subjects is discussed in 2 Peter, but all reaffirm the truthfulness of the apostolic witness and the need to be forewarned of the imminent danger to the testimony by false teachers.

MAJOR CONTENTS
1. Apostolic exhortation (1:2-11)
2. Purposeful progress (1:5-7)
3. Profound priorities (1:8-11)
4. Apostolic testimony (1:12-21)
5. Remembering truth (1:12-15)
6. Observing truth (1:16-21)
7. Apostolic warning (2:1-22)
8. Doctrines of false teachers (2:1-22)
9. Apostolic hope (3:1-18)
10. Doubting the promises (3:1-7)
11. Fulfilling the promises (3:8-10)
12. Living in the light of the promises (3:11-18)

SCRIPTURE MEMORIZATION

2 Pet 1:20: Knowing this first that no _____ of the scripture is of any _____ interpretation.

2 Pet 3:9: The Lord is not _____ concerning his _____, as some men count slackness; but is longsuffering to us-ward, not willing that any should_____, but that all should come to _____ .

190

1 JOHN

A letter written by the same person who wrote one of the Bible's four "biographies" of Jesus. This epistle is a discourse upon the principles of Christianity, in doctrine and practice.

AUTHOR: John the Apostle, the son of Zebedee and the brother of James.

APPROXIMATE DATE: A.D. 80-95. The Epistles of John are usually dated A.D. 80-95. However, the exact date and place cannot be determined with certainty.

THEME: Sound Doctrine, Salvation, and Love

MAJOR CONTENTS
1. The realities of the Christian life (1:1-2:17)
2. Recognizing the word of life (1:1-4)
3. Understanding the character of God (1:5-7)
4. Experiencing a new kind of fellowship (1:8-10)
5. Learning from Jesus (2:1-17)
6. The manifestations of the Christian life (2:18-28)
7. Saints assaulted (2:18-19)
8. Saints anointed (2:20-21)
9. Saints assured (2:22-28)
10. The tests of the Christian life (2:29-3:24)
11. The test of righteousness (2:29-3:12)
12. The test of love (3:13-18)
13. The test of obedience (3:19-24)
14. The assurances of the Christian life (4:1-5:21)
15. A word of instruction (4:1-6)
16. A word of love (4:7-21)
17. A word of faith (5:1-12)
18. A word of victory (5:13-17)
19. A word of confidence (5:18-21)

SCRIPTURE MEMORIZATION

1 John 1:9: If we _____ our sins, he is faithful and just to _____ us our sins, and to cleanse us from all unrighteousness.

1 John 3:4: What is sin? _____

1 John 4:11: Beloved, if God so loved us, we ought also to_____ one another.

2 JOHN

2 John is the shortest book in the Bible. It warns us to watch out for false teachers. First and Second John reflect a comparable background; in each book, the author warns against false teachers and offers encouragement to genuine believers. This is the only book in the Bible addressed to a woman referred to as the "Elect Lady".

AUTHOR: John the Apostle

APPROXIMATE DATE: A.D. 80-95: This epistle was probably penned from Ephesus in A.D. 80-95. However, the date, place, and order of the letters of John cannot be determined with certainty.

THEME: Warning Against False Teachers

MAJOR CONTENTS
1. A new reason for rejoicing (v.4)
2. A new level of life (v.5-6)
3. A new source of danger (v.7)
4. A new basis of appeal (v.8)
5. A new need for watchfulness (v.9-11)

SCRIPTURE MEMORIZATION

2 John 1:6: And this is _____, that we walk after his commandments.

This is the commandment, that, as ye have heard from the _____,

ye should walk in it.

3 JOHN

This is the second shortest book in the Bible. It is a short letter of encouragement.
This epistle is addressed to a converted Gentile. The scope is to commend his steadfastness in the faith, and his hospitality, especially to the ministers of Christ.

AUTHOR: John the Apostle

APPROXIMATE DATE: Along with the first two epistles, the third is dated A.D. 80-95.

THEME: Working Together in Love: The Christian privilege of working together in love is the theme of the epistle

MAJOR CONTENTS

1. A word of appreciation (v. 3-8)
2. A word of denunciation (v. 9-10)
3. A word of instruction (v. 11)
4. A word of praise (v. 12)

SCRIPTURE MEMORIZATION

3 John 1:2: Beloved, I _____above all things that thou mayest

_____ and be in health, even as thy soul prospereth.

3 John 1:11: Beloved, follow not that which is _____, but that which is good. He that

doeth good is of God: but he that doeth evil hath not seen God.

JUDE

The second of two books in the Bible written by a (half) brother of Jesus. This epistle is addressed to all believers in the Gospel. Its purpose was to guard believers against the false teachers who had begun to creep into the Christian church.

AUTHOR: Jude

APPROXIMATE DATE: Uncertain

THEME: Warning Against False Teachers

MAJOR CONTENTS
1. The purpose of the Epistle (v. 3-4)
2. The prophecies of the doom of the ungodly (v. 5-19)
3. Prophecy of Enoch and commentary (v. 14-16)
4. Prophecy of the Apostles and Commentary (v. 17-19)
5. The challenge to Believers (v. 20-23)

SCRIPTURE MEMORIZATION

Jude 1:24-25: Now unto him that is able to keep you from _____, and to present you _____ before the presence of his glory with exceeding _____, To the only wise God our Savior, be glory and _____, dominion and _____, both now and for ever. Amen.

GENERAL EPISTLES
08 BOOKS

APPLIED LEARNING PAGE

WHAT'S THE MISSING BOOK? _____

<u>**RECORD THE AUTHOR**</u>

HEBREWS _____

1 PETER _____

2 PETER _____

1 JOHN _____

2 JOHN _____

3 JOHN _____

JUDE _____

APPLICATION

Write a sentence or song using the first letters of each book to help you memorize the General Epistles.

FUN LEARNING

Apply one of the fun learning techniques from the learning techniques page.

GENERAL EPISTLES
COURSEWORK

HOMEWORK ASSIGNMENTS

QUESTIONS I HAVE FOR A BIBLE TEACHER

SECTION SPECIAL NOTES

PROPHECY
01 BOOK- REVELATION

Revelation is the New Testament's book of prophecy. Revelation's language is very symbolic, which makes it sometimes difficult to understand.

The book of the Revelation consists of two principal divisions:

1. Relates to "the things which are," that is, the then present state of the church, and contains the epistle of John to the seven churches, and his account of the appearance of the Lord Jesus, and his direction to the apostle to write what he beheld, Revelation 1:9-20. Also, addresses the epistles to the seven churches of Asia. These, doubtless, had reference to the state of the respective churches, as they then existed, but contain excellent precepts and exhortations, commendations and reproofs, promises and threatening, suitable to instruct the Christian church at all times.

2. Contains a prophecy of "the things which shall be hereafter," and describes the future state of the church, from the time when the apostle beheld the visions here recorded. It is intended for our spiritual improvement; to warn the careless sinner, point out the way of salvation to the awakened inquirer, build up the weak believer, comfort the afflicted and tempted Christian and we may especially add, to strengthen the martyr of Christ, under the cruel persecutions and sufferings inflicted by Satan and his followers. As an unwelcome forerunner of the earthly fate of Christians in almost every era, the reign of Domitian (A.D. 81-96) burst upon the Roman world at the death of his older brother Titus in A.D. 81. Domitian brought to the imperial office a capacity for intellectual astuteness, bitterness, and conceit. As the latter qualities grew, the cult of Caesar-worship thrived. Jewish communities were likely to suffer; but Christians, with an intense evangelistic advocacy of their new faith, were the inevitable targets of imperial harassment. Earlier persecutions at the hands of both the Jews and Nero (A.D. 64-68) were relatively localized. By the time of the death of Domitian in A.D. 96, many provinces of the empire had reeled under imperial edict.

AUTHOR: John the Apostle

APPROXIMATE DATE: A.D. 90-96

THEME: The End of the Age: "Revelation" The end of earthly life is only the beginning of eternal life. Christians shall spend eternity with God in the New Jerusalem. Unbelievers shall spend eternity with Satan in the lake of fire. God desires that everyone trust in His Son for redemption.

MAJOR CONTENTS

1. Introduction. (1:1-1:8)
2. Christ's revelation of Himself to John. (1:9-1:20)
3. Letters to the seven churches. (2:1-3:22)
4. The throne in Heaven. (4:1-5:14)
5. The seven seals. (6:1-8:5)
6. The seven trumpets. (8:6-11:19)
7. The seven explanatory prophecies. (12:1-14:20)
8. The seven bowls of wrath. (15:1-16:21)
9. The overthrow of Babylon. (17:1-19:6)
10. Prophecies of the second coming of Christ. (19:7-19:21)
11. Prophecies concerning the Millennium. (20:1-20:6)
12. The rebellion and Satan's final doom. (20:7-20:15)
13. The new Heaven and new earth (21:1-22:5)

SCRIPTURE MEMORIZATION

Rev 1:8: I am Alpha and _____, the beginning and the _____, saith the Lord, which _____, and which _____, and which is to come, the Almighty.

Rev 2:29: He that hath an _____, let him hear what the _____ saith unto the churches.

Rev 3:2: Be _____, and strengthen the things which remain, that are ready to _____ for I have not found thy works perfect before God.

Rev 3:20: Behold, I stand at the _____, and _____: if any man hear my _____, and open the door, I will come in to him, and will sup with him, and he with me.

Rev 13:18: What is the number of the beast in revelation? _____

PROPHECY COURSEWORK

HOMEWORK ASSIGNMENTS

QUESTIONS I HAVE FOR A BIBLE TEACHER

SECTION SPECIAL NOTES

APPLIED LEARNING PAGE
BEFORE QUESTIONAIRE

What is the book **before** Proverbs?	
What is the book **before** Philemon?	
What is the book **before** Matthew?	
What is the book **before** Job?	
What is the book **before** Nahum?	
What is the book **before** Ecclesiastes?	
What is the book **before** Hosea?	
What is the book **before** Revelation?	
What is the book **before** Romans?	
What is the book **before** James?	
What is the book **before** Haggai?	
What is the book **before** Acts?	
What is the book **before** 3 John?	
What is the book **before** Lamentations?	
What is the book **before** Leviticus?	
What is the book **before** Nehemiah?	
What is the book **before** 1 Corinthians?	
What is the book **before** Ruth?	
What is the book **before** Psalms?	
What is the book **before** Ephesians?	
What is the book **before** Jeremiah?	
What is the book **before** 1 Chronicles?	
What is the book **before** Micah?	
What is the book **before** 1 Samuel?	
What is the book **before** 1 Thessalonians?	

APPLIED LEARNING PAGE
AFTER QUESTIONAIRE

What is the book **after** 2 Thessalonians?	
What is the book **after** Amos?	
What is the book **after** Ephesians?	
What is the book **after** Titus?	
What is the book **after** Philippians?	
What is the book **after** Esther?	
What is the book **after** Colossians?	
What is the book **after** Romans?	
What is the book **after** Job?	
What is the book **after** Jonah?	
What is the book **after** 2 Samuel?	
What is the book **after** Song of Solomon?	
What is the book **after** Habakkuk?	
What is the book **after** Hebrews?	
What is the book **after** Micah?	
What is the book **after** Ezra?	
What is the book **after** Haggai?	
What is the book **after** 2 Kings?	
What is the book **after** Joel?	
What is the book **after** Jeremiah?	
What is the book **after** Judges?	
What is the book **after** Galatians?	
What is the book **after** 2 Peter?	
What is the book **after** Lamentations?	

WRITE THE AUTHOR OF EACH BOOK

Genesis	_____	Matthew	_____
Exodus	_____	Mark	_____
Leviticus	_____	Luke	_____
Numbers	_____	John	_____
Deuteronomy	_____	Acts	_____
Joshua	_____	Romans	_____
Judges	_____	1 Corinthians	_____
Ruth	_____	2 Corinthians	_____
1 Samuel	_____	Galatians	_____
2 Samuel	_____	Ephesians	_____
1 Kings	_____	Philippians	_____
2 Kings	_____	Colossians	_____
1 Chronicles	_____	1 Thessalonians	_____
2 Chronicles	_____	2 Thessalonians	_____
Ezra	_____	1 Timothy	_____
Nehemiah	_____	2 Timothy	_____
Esther	_____	Titus	_____
Job	_____	Philemon	_____
Psalms	_____	Hebrews	_____
Proverbs	_____	James	_____
Ecclesiastes	_____	1 Peter	_____
Song of Solomon	_____	2 Peter	_____
Isaiah	_____	1 John	_____
Jeremiah	_____	2 John	_____
Lamentations	_____	3 John	_____
Ezekiel	_____	Jude	_____
Daniel	_____	Revelation	_____
Hosea	_____		
Joel	_____		
Amos	_____		
Obadiah	_____		
Jonah	_____		
Micah	_____		
Nahum	_____		
Habakkuk	_____		
Zephaniah	_____		
Haggai	_____		
Zechariah	_____		
Malachi	_____		

NEW TESTAMENT
WHERE IS THE SCRIPTURE?

By now you should have memorized many of the assigned scriptures. Below write down the Book, Chapter and Verse.

In the beginning was the Word, and the Word was with God, and the Word was God.

_____

And I, if I be lifted up from the earth, will draw all men unto me. _____

For all have sinned, and come short of the glory of God. _____

Behold, I stand at the door, and knock: if any man hear my voice, and open the door, I will come in to him, and will sup with him, and he with me. _____

Abstain from all appearance of evil. _____

Stand fast therefore in the liberty wherewith Christ hath made us free, and be not entangled again with the yoke of bondage. _____

And when the day of Pentecost was fully come, they were all with one accord in one place.

_____

But Jesus said unto them, a prophet is not without honor, but in his own country, and among his own kin, and in his own house. _____

Likewise, I say unto you, there is joy in the presence of the angels of God over one sinner that repenteth. _____

But ye shall receive power, after that the Holy Ghost is come upon you: and ye shall be witnesses unto me both in Jerusalem, and in all Judaea, and in Samaria, and unto the uttermost part of the earth. _____

Study to show thyself approved unto God, a workman that needeth not to be ashamed, rightly dividing the word of truth. _____

I can do all things through Christ which strengthened me. _____

But seek ye first the kingdom of God, and his righteousness; and all these things shall be added unto you. _____

NEW TESTAMENT
WHERE IS THE SCRIPTURE?

For God hath not given us the spirit of fear; but of power, and of love, and of a sound mind.

_____

Jesus said unto him, Thou shalt love the Lord thy God with all thy heart, and with all thy soul, and with all thy mind. This is the first and great commandment. And the second is like unto it, Thou shalt love thy neighbor as thyself. On these two commandments hang all the law and the prophets. _____

Go ye therefore, and teach all nations, baptizing them in the name of the Father, and of the Son, and of the Holy Ghost: Teaching them to observe all things whatsoever I have commanded you: and, lo, I am with you always, even unto the end of the world. Amen.

_____

Then Peter said unto them, repent, and be baptized every one of you in the name of Jesus Christ for the remission of sins, and ye shall receive the gift of the Holy Ghost.

_____

There is one body, and one Spirit, even as ye are called in one hope of your calling; One Lord, one faith, one baptism. _____

That at the name of Jesus every knee should bow, of things in heaven, and things in earth, and things under the earth; And that every tongue should confess that Jesus Christ is Lord, to the glory of God the Father. _____

Having a form of godliness, but denying the power thereof. _____

Be watchful, and strengthen the things which remain, that are ready to die: for I have not found thy works perfect before God. _____

And without controversy great is the mystery of godliness: God was manifest in the flesh, justified in the Spirit, seen of angels, preached unto the Gentiles, believed on in the world, received up into glory. _____

But avoid foolish questions, and genealogies, and contentions, and strivings about the law; for they are unprofitable and vain. _____

NEW TESTAMENT
WHERE IS THE SCRIPTURE?

And whether one member suffers, all the members suffer with it; or one member be honored, all the members rejoice with it. _____

That if thou shalt confess with thy mouth the Lord Jesus, and shalt believe in thine heart that God hath raised him from the dead, thou shalt be saved._____

Be ye not unequally yoked together with unbelievers: for what fellowship hath righteousness with unrighteousness? And what communion hath light with darkness? _____

Therefore to him that knoweth to do good and doeth it not, to him it is sin._____

Ye did run well; who did hinder you that ye should not obey the truth?_____

The Lord is not slack concerning his promise, as some men count slackness; but is longsuffering to us-ward, not willing that any should perish, but that all should come to repentance. _____

And if the righteous scarcely be saved, where shall the ungodly and the sinner appear?

_____

For the Son of man is come to seek and to save that which was lost._____

But God commendeth his love toward us, in that, while we were yet sinners, Christ died for us.

_____

Beloved, if God so loved us, we ought also to love one another._____

If we confess our sins, he is faithful and just to forgive us our sins, and to cleanse us from all unrighteousness. _____

That ye be not slothful but followers of them who through faith and patience inherit the promises. _____

Ye have not chosen me, but I have chosen you, and ordained you, that ye should go and bring forth fruit, and that your fruit should remain: that whatsoever ye shall ask of the Father in my name, he may give it you. _____

NEW TESTAMENT
WHERE IS THE SCRIPTURE?

And they said, Believe on the Lord Jesus Christ, and thou shalt be saved, and thy house.

_____

Let not then your good be evil spoken of. _____

Beloved, I wish above all things that thou mayest prosper and be in health, even as thy soul prospereth. _____

I beseech you therefore, brethren, by the mercies of God, that ye present your bodies a living sacrifice, holy, acceptable unto God, which is your reasonable service. And be not conformed to this world: but be ye transformed by the renewing of your mind, that ye may prove what is that good, and acceptable, and perfect, will of God. _____

I am Alpha and Omega, the beginning and the ending, saith the Lord, which is, and which was, and which is to come, the Almighty. _____

For the word of God is quick, and powerful, and sharper than any two edged sword, piercing even to the dividing asunder of soul and spirit, and of the joints and marrow, and is a discerner of the thoughts and intents of the heart. _____

Now unto him that is able to keep you from falling, and to present you faultless before the presence of his glory with exceeding joy, to the only wise God our Savior, be glory and majesty, dominion and power, both now and for ever. Amen. _____

Even so faith, if it hath not works, is dead, being alone. _____

FIND THE MISSING BOOKS
WORKSHEET

WHAT ARE THE TWO MISSING BOOKS?

_____

_____

Matthew
Mark
Luke
John
Acts
1 Corinthians
2 Corinthians
Galatians
Ephesians
Philippians
Colossians
1 Thessalonians
2 Thessalonians

1 Timothy
2 Timothy
Titus
Philemon
James
1 Peter
2 Peter
1 John
2 John
3 John
Jude
Revelation

FIND THE MISSING BOOKS
WORKSHEET

WHAT ARE THE 3 MISSING BOOKS?

_____

_____

_____

Matthew	2 Thessalonians
Mark	1 Timothy
Luke	2 Timothy
John	Titus
Acts	Philemon
Romans	Hebrews
1 Corinthians	1 Peter
2 Corinthians	2 Peter
Galatians	1 John
Ephesians	2 John
Colossians	3 John
1 Thessalonians	Revelation

JOHN 3:16 PUZZLE

```
                    L   U   X   L   T       R
                    E   T   K   A   F       T
                    I   N   H   P   M       H
                    N   T   B   E   I       A
                    A   M   U   X   H       T
                    E   G   J   B   D       N
D   E   E   T   V   S   Q   D   E   V   B   R   A   I   A   A
L   C   Y   P   H   B   G   N   I   T   S   X   L   G   R   E   V   F   E
R   Y   K   E   W   T   G   M   E   F   R   A   I   R   M   E   S   O   E
O   I   E   M   S   L   Z   H   Q   M   X   I   R   E   O   R   F   N   P
W   G   R   L   J   V   L   I   F   E   V   A   O   R   O   F   W   T   E
S   R   E   O   X   J   R   E   N   E   W   E   K   O   H   X   H   I   H
D   H   O   X   J   V   H   N   T   W   R   S   M   K   X   H   C   G   S
J   O   P   N   I   E   S   D   A   Y   P   O   M   V       C       N
                    V   D   T   H   E   S   N
                    A   L   L   T   B   M   V
                    H   T   K   L   E   I   N
                    J   O   H   K   L   M   O
                    K   N   P   H   I   B   Z
                    G   E   G   P   E   S   N
                    B   W   O   G   V   H   P
                    E   L   D   O   E   O   U
                    G   P   N   D   T   U   C
                    O   E   Y   N   H   L   M
                    T   R   L   Y   I   D   S
                    T   I   N   L   F   H   M
                    E   S   O   N   T   F   F
                    N   H   R   O   O   H   S
                    S   U   A   R   C   O   E
                    H       Z   A   Z   Q
```

FIND THESE WORDS

FOR GOD SO LOVED THE WORLD THAT HE GAVE HIS ONLY
BEGOTTEN SON THAT WHOSOEVER BELIEVETH IN HIM SHOULD
NOT PERISH BUT HAVE EVERLASTING LIFE.

NEW TESTAMENT BOOKS

EPH | COL
BOOK BETWEEN?
_____

LUKE | ACTS
BOOK BETWEEN?
_____

3 JOHN | REV
BOOK BETWEEN?
_____

GAL | PHIL
BOOK BETWEEN?
_____

TITUS | HEB
BOOK BETWEEN?
_____

MATT | LUKE
BOOK BETWEEN?
_____

NEW TESTAMENT BOOKS
WORD SEARCH

```
Z L V T G W Z F O L D J M N F W F T N D
X K M U P R R A L I X K F J T E A B V Q
A T C O L O S S I A N S G I B H D T F R
W E E K E M T D T X T V S W R T N U F K
U K K P I A E K E S W S G Q E T U F G K
S C Y H N N W F D V S T J Q T A X K D P
O G H I E S V N Q C P A V J E M H N K O
Z G J L Z T I M O T H Y X W P I E O S Y
A A E E S B W T L N J P K X F T B M U J
C L K M V V Q A Y T O N X Z Q X R U T Q
T A U O F B V D C M H J R H N R E X I J
S T L N J J M G I U N N A F H N W Q T L
F I D Y F W N Y B F F B I M S A S Y Y D
Y A S M O G M F I Z H Z U N E C Q W L E
F N Z S P E E P H E S I A N S S J D G Y
I S V T H E S S A L O N I A N S R O E G
M W C I C R F V N O I T A L E V E R I F
G Y O S N A I P P I L I H P B D F E B X
U S N A I H T N I R O C Y O B P J U D E
B A V E Y R A L X Q W Y M C J K R A M D
```

FIND THESE WORDS

Acts	Colossians	Corinthians	Ephesians	Galatians	Hebrews	James
John	Jude	Luke	Mark	Matthew	Peter	Philemon
Philippians	Revelation	Romans	Thessalonians	Timothy	Titus	

GENERAL BIBLE
APPLIED LEARNING PAGE

1. How many books are in the Bible? _____

2. How many books are in the Old Testament? _____

3. How many books are in the New Testament? _____

4. Which book would you look for the Sermon on the Mount? _____

5. In which book would you look for the story of Jonah and the great fish? _____

6. How many of the New Testament books are called the Gospels?_____

7. Which is the shortest Gospel book?_____

8. In what book of the Bible would you read about the 3 Hebrew boys?_____

9. Which book includes the story of the Tower of Babel?_____

10. Which 2 books records the 10 Commandments?_____

11. How many NT books are called Pauline Epistles? _____

12. List the three Pastoral Epistles. _____

13. How many NT books are called General Epistles?_____

14. Which NT book is the only book with an unknown author? _____

WHO IS JESUS
IN THE NEW TESTAMENT

In Matthew	He is king of the Jews
In Mark	He is the servant
In Luke	He is the Son of Man, feeling what you feel
In John	He is the Son of God
In Acts	He is Savior of the world
In Romans	He is the righteousness of God
In 1 Corinthians	He is the rock that followed Israel
In 2 Corinthians	He the triumphant one, giving victory
In Galatians	He is your liberty; He sets you free
In Ephesians	He is head of the Church
In Philippians	He is your joy
In Colossians	He is your completeness
In 1 and 2 Thessalonians	He is your hope
In 1 Timothy	He is your faith
In 2 Timothy	He is your stability
In Titus	He is your guide
In Philemon	He is your benefactor
In Hebrews	He is your perfection
In James	He is the power behind your faith
In 1 Peter	He is your example
In 2 Peter	He is your purity
In 1 John	He is your life
In 2 John	He is your pattern
In 3 John	He is your motivation
In Jude	He is the foundation of your faith
In Revelation	He is your coming King

SHORT SUMMARY
OF THE 66 BIBLE BOOKS

Genesis	Creation, the Fall, and Israel's Birth
Exodus	Leaving Egypt and Getting the Law
Leviticus	Priestly Laws
Numbers	Israel's Census and Wandering in the Wilderness
Deuteronomy	Retelling of the Law
Joshua	Conquering Canaan
Judges	Cycles of Spiritual Freedom and Political Bondage
Ruth	A Gentile Marries Into the Davidic Lineage
1 Samuel	Israel's Kingdom Instituted
2 Samuel	David Reigns
1 Kings	The Kingdom Splits Israel and Judah)
2 Kings	The Divided Kingdom Struggles
1 Chronicles	David's Reign Retold
2 Chronicles	Judah's Evil Leads to Babylonian Captivity
Ezra	A Remnant Returns to Rebuild the Temple
Nehemiah	More Return to Restore Jerusalem's Walls and Life
Esther	Jews in Persia Saved from Extermination
Job	A Righteous Man Labors to Understand Suffering
Psalms	Israel's Hymnal
Proverbs	Solomon's Wise Sayings
Ecclesiastes	Backslidden Solomon's Confusion
Song of Solomon	Romance Portrays God's Love for Israel
Isaiah	The Coming Messiah will Suffer and Rule
Jeremiah	A Second Captivity Left Behind the Prophet
Lamentations	Israel's Divorce Decree from God
Ezekiel	In Exile, Explaining Israel's Judgment and Hope
Daniel	Vision of God Conquering Gentile Kingdoms
Hosea	Northern Israel's Sin Leads to Assyrian Captivity
Joel	In the Great Tribulation God will Pour Out His Spirit
Amos	Renaissance Israel to Fall Before Messiah Comes
Obadiah	God will Destroy Edom
Jonah	A Reluctant Prophet Converts the Assyrian Capital
Micah	Doom Coming
Nahum	The Destruction of Nineveh Predicted
Habakkuk	The Just Shall Live by Faith
Zephaniah	Judah's Superficial Repentance
Haggai	Judgment for the Delay of Rebuilding the Temple
Zechariah	Temple Rebuilt
Malachi	Repent! Prepare the Way of the Lord

SHORT SUMMARY
OF THE 66 BIBLE BOOKS

Matthew	King Jesus, Son of David
Mark	Jesus the Servant, with No Genealogy
Luke	Jesus the Man, Son of Adam
John	God Became Flesh
Acts	Peter's Ministry Wanes
Romans	Paul's Theological Treatise
1 Corinthians	Correcting the Body of Christ
2 Corinthians	Defense of Paul's Apostleship
Galatians	Paul's Gospel of Grace over Peter's Legalism
Ephesians	The Dispensation of Grace Given to Paul
Philippians	The Resurrection Yields Joy in Suffering
Colossians	God Nailed the Law to the Cross for Our Victory
1 Thessalonians	Knowing that the Lord will Return
2 Thessalonians	The Great Tribulation Had Not Yet Arrived
1 Timothy	The Proper Administration of the Body of Christ
2 Timothy	Paul Encourages Timothy to Persevere
Titus	Appointment of Elders for Orderly Church
Philemon	The Conversion and Return of a Runaway Slave
Hebrews	The Epistle to the Hebrews
James	Jews of the Twelve Tribes of Israel Urged to Works
1 Peter	Believing Jews of the Dispersion Were Suffering
2 Peter	Peter's Converts Urged to Not Fall Away
1 John	John's Converts Must Confess their Sins
2 John	Truth Can Keep John's Converts from Deception
3 John	Israel Warned Not to Take Anything from Gentiles
Jude	Warning Against Apostasy
Revelation	God Judges Man

FACTS ON THE BIBLE

1. How many books are in the Bible?
   The Bible contains 66 books, divided among the Old and New Testaments.

2. How many books are in the Old Testament?
   There are 39 books in the Old Testament.

3. How many books are in the New Testament?
   There are 27 books in the New Testament.

4. Who wrote the Bible?
   The Bible was written under the inspiration of the Holy Spirit by over 40 different authors.

5. Which single author contributed the most books to the Old Testament?
   Moses. He wrote the first five books of the Bible, referred to as the Law.

6. Which single author contributed the most books to the New Testament?
   The Apostle Paul, who wrote 13 books.

7. What languages was the Bible written in?
   The Bible was written in three languages: Hebrew, Aramaic, and Greek.

8. What is the longest book in the Bible?
   The book of Psalms has the most chapters.
   The book of Jeremiah has the most words.

9. What is the shortest book in the Bible?
   2 John is the shortest book in the Bible.
   Obadiah has only one chapter and is the shortest OT book.

10. What is the longest chapter in the Bible?
   Psalms 119

FACTS ON THE BIBLE

11. What is the shortest chapter in the Bible?
Psalms 117

12. What is the longest verse in the Bible?
Esther 8:9

13. What is the shortest verse in the Bible?
John 11:35   (Jesus Wept.)

14. Which books in the Bible does not mention the word "God?"
The book of Esther.
The book of Song of Solomon.

15. Who was the oldest man that ever lived?
Methuselah who lived to be 969 years old (Genesis 5:27).

16. Who were the two men in the Bible who never died but were caught up to heaven?
Enoch, who walked with God and was no more (Genesis 5:22-24).
Elijah, who was caught up by a whirlwind into heaven (2 Kings 2:11).

17. Who does the Bible say was the meekest man in the Bible (not including Jesus)?
Moses (Numbers 12:3).

18. How may silent years between the Old and New Testament?
400 years.

19. Approximately how long did it take the 40 authors to write the Bible?
Approximately 1600 years.

20. Which is the only book in the Bible written to a Woman (Elect Lady)?
2 John.

GREAT CHAPTERS

Creation	Genesis 1:1–2:7
Passover	Exodus 12
Commandments	Exodus 20
God's Love	Psalms 23
Forgiveness	Psalms 51
God's Laws	Psalms 119
God's Knowledge	Psalms 139
Wisdom	Proverbs 1–2
A Good Wife	Proverbs 31:10-30
A Time for Everything	Ecclesiastes 3
The Suffering Servant	Isaiah 52:13–53:12
Jesus on the Mountainside	Matthew 5–7
Greatest Commandment	Mark 12:28-34
Parable of the Lost Son	Luke 15:11-32
Eternal Life	John 1, 3
The Holy Spirit	John 14:15-17
The Holy Spirit Comes	Acts 2
Salvation	Romans 3
Love	1 Corinthians 13
Spiritual Armor	Ephesians 6:10-20
Right Living	Colossians 3
Leadership	1 Timothy 3
Faith	Hebrews 11
Temptation	James 1
Suffering	1 Peter 4
Fellowship	1 John 1
Heaven	Revelation 21–22

GREAT OLD TESTAMENT STORIES

Cain and Abel	Genesis 4:1-16
The Flood	Genesis 6:1–9:17
The Tower of Babel	Genesis 11:1-9
Abraham's Obedience	Genesis 12:1-9
Sacrifice of Isaac	Genesis 22:1-19
Joseph and a Coat	Genesis 37:1-36; 39:1–23
Moses Is Born	Exodus 2:1-10
The Burning Bush	Exodus 3:1-22
The Ten Plagues	Exodus 7:14–12:30
The Exodus	Exodus 12:31-51
Crossing the Red Sea	Exodus 14:15-31
The Gold Calf	Exodus 32:1-29
Spies into Canaan	Numbers 13:1-33
The Bronze Snake	Numbers 21:4-9
Battle of Jericho	Joshua 6:1-27
Gideon as Judge	Judges 6:1–7:25
Samson as Judge	Judges 13:1–16:31
God Provides for Ruth	Ruth 1:1–4:22
Samuel Is Born	1 Samuel 1:1-28
David Kills Goliath	1 Samuel 17:1-51
David and Jonathan	1 Samuel 18:1-4; 20:1-42
David and Bathsheba	2 Samuel 11:1-27
Solomon Judges Wisely	1 Kings 3:16-28
Elijah-the Prophets of Baal	1 Kings 18:1-40
God Speaks to Elijah	1 Kings 19:1-18
Elisha Heals Naaman	2 Kings 5:1-19
David's Mighty Men	1 Chronicles 11:10-25
Esther Saves the Jews	Esther 1:1–10:3
Job Is Tested	Job 1:1-22; Job 2:1-13
Ezekiel's Vision	Ezekiel 37:1-14
The Fiery Furnace	Daniel 3:1-30
The Lion's Den	Daniel 6:1-28
Jonah and the Fish	Jonah 1:1–2:10

GREAT NEW TESTAMENT STORIES

Jesus is Born	Matthew 1:18-25
	Luke 2:1-20
Wise Men Visit Jesus	Matthew 2:1-12
Baptism of Jesus	Matthew 3:13-17
Jesus is tempted	Matthew 4:1-11
	Mark 1:12-13
	Luke 4:1-13
Jesus Feeds Five Thousand	Matthew 14:13-21
	Mark 6:30-44
	Luke 9:10-17
	John 6:1-15
Jesus Walks on Water	Matthew 14:22-33
	Mark 6:45-52
	John 6:16-21
The Great Commission	Matthew 28:16-20
The Good Samaritan	Luke 10:25-37
The Lost Son	Luke 15:11-32
Jesus Raises Lazarus	John 11:1-44
Jesus Enters Jerusalem	Matthew 21:1-11
	Luke 19:28-40
	John 12:12-19
The Last Supper	Matthew 26:17-30
	Mark 14:12-26
	Luke 22:7-30
	John 13:1-30
Jesus' Execution	Matthew 27:32-56
	Mark 15:21-41
	Luke 23:26-49
	John 19:16-37
Jesus' Resurrection	Matthew 28:1-15
	Mark 16:1-14
	Luke 24:1-12
	John 20:1-10
Jesus Goes into Heaven	Luke 24:50-53
	Acts 1:6-11
The Holy Spirit	Acts 2:1-13
Ananias and Sapphira	Acts 5:1-11
Saul Encounters Jesus	Acts 9:1-19
Paul is Shipwrecked	Acts 27:1–28:10

UNUSUAL THINGS IN THE BIBLE

✞ Male and females both being called Adam, referring to mankind (Genesis 5:1-2).

✞ Man who lived to be 969 years old (Genesis 5:27).

✞ Sons of God married the daughters of men (Genesis 6:2).

✞ Man used a stone for a pillow (Genesis 28:11).

✞ Baby had a scarlet thread tied around its hand before it was born (Genesis 38:28-29).

✞ Battle won because a man stretched out his hand (Exodus 17:11).

✞ Man was spoken to by a donkey (Numbers 22:28-30).

✞ One who had a bed 13½ feet long and 6 feet wide (Deuteronomy 3:11).

✞ The women who had to shave their heads before marriage (Deuteronomy 21:11-13).

✞ Sun stood still for a whole day (Joshua 10:13).

✞ An army with 700 left handed men (Judges 20:16).

✞ King Saul and, his son-in-law, King David both had wives named Ahinoam
(1 Samuel 14:50; 1 Samuel 25:43; 1 Samuel 30:5; 2 Samuel 2:2).

✞ The giant Goliath was 9 ½ feet tall (1 Samuel 17:4).

✞ Man whose hair weighed about 6 pounds when it was cut annually (2 Samuel 14:26).

✞ Man who had 12 fingers and 12 toes (2 Samuel 21:20 and 1 Chronicles 20:6).

✞ Father who had eighty-eight children (2 Chronicles 11:21).

✞ The sun traveled backward (Isaiah 38:8).

✞ A harlot was an ancestor of Christ (Matthew 1:5).

✞ Besides Noah who built the Ark, there is a woman in the Bible named Noah
(Numbers 26:33; Numbers 27:1; Numbers 36:10-11).

COMPOUND NAMES OF JEHOVAH

	NAME	SCRIPTURE	MEANING
1	Jehovah-jireh	Genesis 22:14	The LORD will provide
2	Jehovah-rapha	Exodus 15:26	The LORD that heals
3	Jehovah-nissi	Exodus 17:15	The LORD our banner (victory)
4	Jehovah-m'kaddesh	Exodus 31:13	The LORD that sanctifies
5	Jehovah-shalom	Judges 6:24	The LORD our peace
6	Jehovah-sabaoth	I Samuel 1:3	The LORD of hosts (almighty)
7	Jehovah-elyon	Psalms 7:17	The LORD most high
8	Jehovah-raah	Psalms 23:1	The LORD my shepherd
9	Jehovah-hoseenu	Psalms 95:6	The LORD our maker
10	Jehovah-tsidkenu	Jeremiah 23:6	The LORD our righteousness
11	Jehovah-shammah	Ezekiel 48:35	The LORD is present

OLD TESTAMENT NAMES FOR GOD

	ENGLISH	HEBREW	SCRIPTURE
1	God	Elohim	Genesis 1:1
2	God	El	Genesis 14:18
3	God	Eloah	Nehemiah 9:17
4	God	Elah	Daniel 2:18
5	God	Yahweh	Genesis 15:2
6	Lord	YHWH or YH	Genesis 2:4
7	Jehovah	YHWH	Exodus 6:3
8	JAH	YH (Yah)	Psalms 68:4
9	Lord	Adon	Joshua 3:11
10	Lord	Adonai	Genesis 15:2
11	I Am That I Am	Eheyeh	Exodus 3:14
12	Most High God	El-Elyon	Genesis 14:18
13	The God of sight	El-Roiy	Genesis 16:13
14	Almighty God	El-Shaddai	Genesis 17:1
15	Everlasting God	El-Olam	Genesis 21:33

TITLES OF CHRIST

NAME OR TITLE	SIGNIFICANCE	BIBLICAL
Adam, Last Adam	First of the new race of the redeemed	1 Corinthians 15:45
Alpha and Omega	The beginning and ending of all things	Revelation 21:6
Bread of Life	The one essential food	John 6:35
Chief Cornerstone	A sure foundation for life	Ephesians 2:20
Chief Shepherd	Protector, sustainer, and guide	1 Peter 5:4
Firstborn from the Dead	Leads us into resurrection and eternal life	Colossians 1:18
Good Shepherd	Provider and caretaker	John 10:11
Great Shepherd	Trustworthy guide and protector	Hebrews 13:20
High Priest	A perfect sacrifice for our sins	Hebrews 3:1
Holy One of God	Sinless is His nature	Mark 1:24
Immanuel (God With Us)	Stands with us in all of life's circumstances	Matthew 1:23
King of Kings Lord of Lords	The Almighty, before whom every knee will bow	Revelation 19:16
Lamb of God	Gave His life as a sacrifice on our behalf	John 1:29
Light of the World	Brings hope in the midst of darkness	John 9:5
Lord of Glory	The power and presence of the living God	1 Corinthians 2:8
Mediator between God and Man	Brings us into God's presence redeemed and forgiven	1 Timothy 2:5
Only Begotten of the Father	The unique, one-of-a kind Son of God	John 1:14
Prophet	Faithful proclaimed of the truths of God	Acts 3:22
Savior	Delivers from sin and death	Luke 1:47
Seed of Abraham	Mediator of God's covenant	Galatians 3:16
Son of Man	Identifies with us in our humanity	Matthew 18:11
The Word	Was present with God at the creation	John 1:1

MEANING OF BIBLE NAMES

Names of people in The Bible often have very interesting meanings from the original languages. Here are a few examples:

BIBLE NAME	MEANING
Abel	Breath, acquired
Abraham	Father of a multitude
Adam	Mankind or human being
Amos	Burden-Bearer
Andrew	A strong man, manly
Barabbas	Son of shame, son of the father, teacher
Barnabas	Son of Encouragement
Boaz	Strength, might, quickness
Cain	Brought forth, to acquire, possession
Dan	Judgment, he that judges
Daniel	God is my judge
David	Well-beloved
Delilah	Temptress, small
Dinah	Justice
Eli	Uplifted
Elijah	God is the Lord, My God is Yahweh
Elisha	God is salvation
Enoch	Dedicated One, Follower
Ephraim	Fruitful
Esau	Hairy, He that acts or finishes
Esther	Star
Eve	Mother, Life-giving
Ezekiel	Strength of God
Felix	Happy
Gabriel	God is my strength-warrior, Strong man of God
Gideon	He that bruises or breaks, a destroyer, cutter
Habakkuk	Embracer or wrestler
Hezekiah	The Lord has strengthened
Hosea	Savior, safety
Immanuel	God is with us
Isaac	Laughter, He laughed
Isaiah	Salvation of the Lord
Ishmael	God hears
Jabez	Sorrow, trouble
Jacob	Supplanter, my God protects, undermines

Jazeel	Strength of God
Jehoshaphat	The Lord has judged
Jeremiah	Exaltation of the Lord
Job	He that weeps or cries, persecuted one
John	The Lord has been gracious, the mercy of the Lord
Jonah	Dove, he that oppresses, destroyer
Jonathan	Given of God
Joseph	God add, increase, addition
Judah	Praise
Lazarus	God has helped, assistance of God
Leah	Weary, tired
Lo-ruhamah	Not loved or not pitied
Lot	Covering, concealed
Luke	Beloved, Light
Malachi	My messenger, my angel
Manasseh	Forgetfulness, he that forgets
Mary	God's gift, Bitterness
Melchizedek	King of righteousness
Moses	Drawn out, taken out
Naomi	Beautiful, agreeable, pleasant
Nebuchadnezzar	Tears, groans of judgment, protect my boundary
Nehemiah	Yahweh comforts, repentance of the Lord
Nicodemus	Victory of the people, conqueror of the people
Noah	Comfort, to rest
Obadiah	Servant of the Lord
Peter	Rock
Phoebe	Pure, bright or radiant
Raphael	God heals
Ruth	Companion, friend or being satisfied
Samuel	Heard of God, asked of God
Sarah	Princess lady, princess of the multitude
Saul	The one asking, demanding
Simeon	One who hears or obeys
Solomon	Peaceful, prosperity
Stephen	Crown
Timotheus	Honor of God, valued of God
Uriah	The Lord is my light or fire
Uzzah	God is my strength
Vashti	The beloved desired one, beautiful woman
Zacchaeus	Pure, clean, just, righteous
Zephaniah	The Lord is my secret

NUMBERS OF THE BIBLE

These numbers are NOT for the study of numerology but rather for Bible Study in understanding how certain numbers have a spiritual meaning. Throughout the Scriptures there are obvious references to specific numbers.

NUMBER	DESCRIPTION	SCRIPTURE	OTHER OBSERVATIONS
One	Beginning, Unison, Oneness of God	Genesis 1 John 5:7 Deuteronomy 6:4	There is one true God. The Father, the Word and the Holy Spirit are one.
Two	Unity, Witness Separation, Division	Matthew 18:16 Genesis 1:27 Deuteronomy 17:6 John 8:17 1 Kings 18:21 Matthew 7:13-14	In the mouth of two or three witnesses. The Bible is divided into two testaments (old and new)
Three	Completion, Testing Trinity of God, Resurrection	1 Corinthians13:13 Judges 7:16 Matthew 28:19 2 Corinthians 13:14 Hosea 6:1-2 Matthew 12:40 Luke 13:32	Father, Son, Holy Spirit Spirit, Soul, and Body Yesterday, Today, Tomorrow Animal, Vegetable, Mineral Beginning, middle, end
Four	Earth, Creation, World Breath of God, The four seasons, Sowing and Reaping	Genesis 2:10 Ezekiel 37:9 John 4:35 Matthew 13:4-8	The four elements The four directions The four seasons The four divisions of the day The four basic operations of math
Five	Grace, Cross, Atonement, Wisdom, Ministry, Good Stewardship	Matthew 25:2 Ephesians 4:11 Matthew 25:15	The favor of God's grace God informed Paul, His grace was sufficient.
Six	Man and Beast	Genesis 1:26-31	The earth was prepared for man in six days.
Seven	Perfection Completeness Rest Fulfillment	Exodus 20:11 Exodus 20:10 Joshua 6:4	7 days make a complete week 7 colors = a perfect spectrum 7 land masses = earth 7 notes = a perfect scale 7 bodies of water = a ocean 7 days of creation

NUMBERS OF THE BIBLE

UMBER	DESCRIPTION	SCRIPTURE	OTHER OBSERVATIONS
ght	New Beginning	1 Peter 3:20-22	Circumcision was to be on the eighth day.
ine	Finality, fullness Fruits and Gifts	Galatians 5:22 1 Cor.12:1-12	The number nine consists of 3 x 3. It is the completeness of completeness.
en	Law, government, restoration God's Commandments	Exodus 20:1-17	The Ten Commandments One tenth = The Tithe
even	Confusion, disorganization	Genesis 9:20 Genesis 10:15-18	After Judas' betrayal, there were only 11 apostles. Before the Holy Spirit could come on the Day of Pentecost, the twelfth apostle had to be appointed.
welve	Divine Government, Apostolic fullness	Rev 21:12-17 Genesis 49:28 Matthew 10:2-4 Rev. 12:1	The twelve apostles. The twelve tribes of Israel.
hirteen	Rebellion, backsliding	Mark 7:21 1 Kings 7:1	Israel rebelled against God thirteen times in the wilderness.
66	Satan, the Antichrist	Rev 13:18	666 is the number of the beast, the great antichrist.

COLORS OF THE BIBLE

COLOR	MEANING	SCRIPTURE
Amber	Symbolizes the Glory of God. God's Anointing-Consecration.	Ezekiel 1: 28 Exodus 29:7
Black	The color black symbolizes sin, death, depression, and famine. Nowadays the color black has taken on a different meaning and may represent sophistication; elegance, dignity and honor (Judges and clergy members often wear black robes).	Job 3:5; 10:20-22; 30:26; Psalms 107:10,11; 143:3; Isaiah 5:30; 8:22; 9:19; 24:11; 50:3; Joel 2:6,10; 3:14,15; Amos 5:8; Nahum 2:10; Zephaniah 1:14,15; Matthew 8:12; 22:13; 25:30; 2 Peter 2:4; Jude 1:13; Revelation 16:10

COLORS OF THE BIBLE

COLOR	MEANING	SCRIPTURE
Blue	Used to describe the sky, Heaven, the Holy Spirit and authority.	Exodus 24:10; 25:3,4; 26:1; 28:28,37; 38:18; 39:1-5,21,24,29,31; Numbers 4:5-12; 15:38-40; 2 Chronicles 2:7-14; 3:14; Jeremiah 10:9; Ezekiel 1:26; 10:1
Brown	A dark, blackish color referred only to sheep. Flesh.	A dark, blackish color referred only sheep (Genesis 30:32-40).
Crimson	Often refers to blood atonement and sacrifice.	Crimson linen was used in the temple (2 Chronicles 2:7, 14, 3:14); the color must have been permanent (Jeremiah 4:30), as crimson is used figuratively as sin. (Isaiah 1:18).
Gray	Describe the hair of the elderly. Dignity, honor, age.	Used to describe the hair of the elderly (Genesis 42:38)
Green	Most often associated with the meaning of growth. Also represent healing and prosperity.	Normally describes vegetation; used of pastures (Psalms 23:2); trees in general (Deuteronomy 12:2; Luke 23:31; Revelation 8:7); the marriage bed (in a figurative sense, Song of Solomon 1:16); a hypocrite compared to a papyrus plant (Job 8:16); and grass (Mark 6:39). A word meaning "greenish" describes plague spots (Leviticus 13:49, 14:37) as well as the color of gold.
Gold	Kingdom glory. Wealth.	Exodus 28:36; 1 Kings 6:21; Rev. 21:18
Purple	This color symbolizes kingship and royalty.	The most precious of ancient dyes made from a shellfish found in the Mediterranean Sea. A total of 250,000 mollusks were required to make one ounce of the dye, which partly accounts for its great price. It was highly valued within the nation of Israel. Used in several features of the tabernacle (Exodus 26:1; Exodus 27:16) and the temple (2 Chronicles 2:14); the color of royal robes (Judges 8:26); the garments of the wealthy (Proverbs 31:22; Luke 16:19); the vesture of a harlot (Revelation 17:4); and the robe placed on Jesus (Mark 15:17-20).

228

COLORS OF THE BIBLE

COLOR	MEANING	SCRIPTURE
Rainbow	God's Promises Covenant.	Revelation 4:3; Genesis 9:13-16
Red	The color of blood, it often symbolizes life; it also suggests bloodshed.	Describes natural objects such as Jacob's stew (Genesis 25:30); the sacrificial heifer (Numbers 19:2); wine (Proverbs 23:31); newborn Esau (Genesis 25:25); Judah's eyes (Genesis 49:12); the eyes of the drunkard (Proverbs 23:29); and the dragon (Revelation 12:3).
Scarlet	Often refers to blood atonement and sacrifice.	Scarlet cord was tied around the wrist of Zerah (Genesis 38:28-30); used a great deal in the tabernacle (Exodus 25:4); the color of cord hung from Rahab's window (Joshua 2:18); a mark of prosperity (2 Samuel 1:24; Proverbs 31:21); the color of the robe placed on Jesus (Matthew 27:28); though scarlet and purple were not always distinguished (Mark 15:17); color of the beast ridden by the harlot Babylon (Revelation 17:3) along with some of her garments (Revelation 17:4) and those of her followers (Revelation 18:16).
Silver	Redemption.	Matthew 27:3-9
White	Portrays purity, innocence, righteousness, joy, light, and victory. An Overcomer.	The high priest's holy garments were made of white linen (Leviticus 16:4,32) Choir singers were arrayed in white (2 Chronicles 5:12; Revelation 2:17)
Yellow	Indicates the greenish cast of gold. The Shekinah Glory.	Psalms 68:13; Leviticus 13:30-32; Revelation 21:23; Matthew 17:2

SICKNESSES IN THE BIBLE

Luke was a Physician in Bible times. Colossians 4:14: "Luke, the beloved physician, and Demas, greet you." There are several recorded illnesses in the Bible. To name just a few:

SICKNESS	SOME OF THE SCRIPTURES
Barren	Genesis 15:2; Genesis 17; Genesis 20:17; Genesis 21
Blindness	Matthew 9:27-30; Matthew 20:30; Mark 8:22-23; Mark 10:46-51; Luke 18:35; John 9:1-41; Acts 9:1-9
Man with Bloody Discharge	Acts 28:8
Bent Over	Luke 13:11-13
Boils	Exodus 9:9-11; 2 Kings 20:7; Job 2:7
Bowels Falling Out	2 Chronicles 21:15-19
Broken Foot, Broken Hand, crookbacked, or a dwarf	Leviticus 21:16-20
Broken Heart	Psalms 34:18; Luke 4:18
Crippled or Lame	John 5:1-8; Acts 3:1-11
Deaf	Leviticus 19:14; Mark 9:25-26
Dumbness	Mark 9:25-26
Eyes Dim (vision problems)	1 Samuel 4:15
Foot Disease	1 Kings 15:23; 2 Chronicles 16:12
High Fevers	Deut. 28:22; Matthew 8:14-15; Mark 1:30-31; Acts 28:8
Inflammation	Deuteronomy 28:22
Issue of Blood	Matthew 9:20; Mark 5:25; Luke 8:43-44
Knee and Leg Problems	Deuteronomy 28:35
Leprosy	Leviticus 13 1-59; 2 Chronicles 26:20-23; Luke 5:12-16
Menstruation	Leviticus 15:33; Leviticus 20:18
Obesity or Heaviness	Judges 3:17-22; 1 Samuel 4:18
Palsy	Matthew 8:6; Luke 5:18; Acts 9:32-35
Demon Possession	Matthew 12:22; Mark 1:32-39; several other scriptures
Stroke	Ezekiel 24:16

James 5:14-15: Is any sick among you? Let him call for the elders of the church; and let them pray over him, anointing him with oil in the name of the Lord: And the prayer of faith shall save the sick, and the Lord shall raise him up; and if he has committed sins, they shall be forgiven him.

Isaiah 53:5: But he was wounded for our transgressions, he was bruised for our iniquities: the chastisement of our peace was upon him; and with his stripes we are healed.

AGES AT DEATH

AGE AT DEATH	WHO	SCRIPTURE
969 years old at death	Methuselah	Genesis 5:27: And all the days of Methuselah were nine hundred sixty and nine years and he died.
962 years old at death	Jared	Genesis 5:20: And all the days of Jared were nine hundred sixty and two years and he died.
950 years old at death	Noah	Genesis 9:29: And all the days of Noah were nine hundred and fifty years and he died.
930 years Old at death	Adam	Genesis 5:5: And all the days that Adam lived was nine hundred and thirty years and he died.
912 years old at death	Seth	Genesis 5:8: And all the days of Seth were nine hundred and twelve years and he died.
910 years old at death	Cainan	Genesis 5:14: And all the days of Cainan were nine hundred and ten years and he died.
905 years old at death	Enos	Genesis 5:11: And all the days of Enos were nine hundred and five years and he died.
825 years old at death	Mahalaleel	Genesis 5:17: And all the days of Mahalaleel were eight hundred ninety and five years and he died.
777 years old at death	Lamech	Genesis 5:31: And all the days of Lamech were seven hundred seventy and seven years and he died.
600 years old at death	Shem	Genesis 11:10-11: These are the generations of Shem: Shem was an hundred years old, and begat Arphaxad two years after the flood and Shem lived after he begat Arphaxad five hundred years, and begat sons and daughters.
464 years old at death	Eber	Genesis 11:16-17: And Eber lived four and thirty years, and begat Peleg and Eber lived after he begat Peleg four hundred and thirty years, and begat sons and daughters.
438 years old at death	Arphaxad	Genesis 11:12-13: And Arphaxad lived five and thirty years, and begat Salah and Arphaxad lived after he begat Salah four hundred and three years.
433 years old at death	Salah	Genesis 11:14-15: And Salah lived thirty years, and begat Eber and Salah lived after he begat Eber four hundred and three years, and begat sons and daughters.
205 years old at death	Terah	Genesis 11:32: And the days of Terah were two hundred and five years and Terah died in Haran. (This was Abraham's father)

AGES AT DEATH

180 years old at death	Isaac	Genesis 35:28: And the days of Isaac were an hundred and fourscore years.
175 years old at death	Abraham	Genesis 25:7: And these are the days of the years of Abraham's life which he lived, an hundred threescore and fifteen years.
147 years old at death	Jacob	Genesis 49: Jacob, having blessed his sons and the sons of Joseph, Ephraim and Manasseh, dies at 147 years old. Gen. 49:33: And when Jacob had made an end of commanding his sons, he gathered up his feet into the bed, and yielded up the ghost, and was gathered unto his people.
130 years old at death	Jehoiada	2 Chronicles 24:15: But Jehoiada waxed old, and was full of days when he died; an hundred and thirty years old was he when he died.
127 years old at death	Sarah	Genesis 23:1-2: And Sarah was an hundred and seven and twenty years old: these were the years of the life of Sarah. And Sarah died in Kirjatharba; the same is Hebron in the land of Canaan: and Abraham came to mourn for Sarah, and to weep for her.
123 years old at death	Aaron	Numbers 33:39: And Aaron was an hundred and twenty and three years old when he died in Mount Hor.
120 years old at death	Moses	Deuteronomy 34:5-7: So Moses the servant of the LORD died there in the land of Moab, according to the word of the LORD. And he buried him in a valley in the land of Moab, over against Bethpeor: but no man knoweth of his sepulchre unto this day. And Moses was an hundred and twenty years old when he died: his eye was not dim, nor his natural force abated.
110 years old at death	Joseph	Genesis 50:26: So Joseph died, being an hundred and ten years old: and they embalmed him, and he was put in a coffin in Egypt.
110 years old at death	Joshua	Joshua 24:29: And it came to pass after these things, that Joshua the son of Nun, the servant of the LORD, died, being an hundred and ten years old.
98 years old at death	Eli	The report that his sons Hophni and Phinehas were dead, and the ark of God was taken (1 Samuel 4:12-18). Eli fell backwards from off his seat, broke his neck and died, being ninety and eight years old. He was stated as being a 'heavy' man.

AGES AT DEATH

70 years old at death	David	David was thirty years old when he began to reign, and he reigned forty years. (2 Samuel 5:4). 1 Kings 2:1-2: Now the days of David drew nigh that he should die; and he charged Solomon his son, saying, I go the way of all the earth: be thou strong therefore, and show thyself a man. 1 Kings 2:10-12: So David slept with his fathers, and was buried in the city of David. And the days that David reigned over Israel were forty years: seven years reigned he in Hebron, and thirty and three years reigned he in Jerusalem. Then sat Solomon upon the throne of David his father; and his kingdom was established greatly.

Psalm 90:10: The days of **OUR YEARS** are **THREESCORE YEARS AND TEN**; and if by reason of strength they be fourscore years, yet is their strength labor and sorrow; for it is soon cut off, and we fly away.

A Score represents 20 years. Threescore and ten is: (20 x 3 = 60 + 10= 70 years).

Philippians 1:21-23: For to me to live is Christ, and to die is gain. For to me to live is Christ, and to die is gain. But if I live in the flesh, this is the fruit of my labor: yet what I shall choose I wot not. For I am in a strait betwixt two, having a desire to depart, and to be with Christ; which is far better.

1 Corinthians 15:51-57: Behold, I show you a mystery; we shall not all sleep, but we shall all be changed, In a moment, in the twinkling of an eye, at the last trump: for the trumpet shall sound, and the dead shall be raised incorruptible, and we shall be changed. For this corruptible must put on incorruption, and this mortal must put on immortality. So when this corruptible shall have put on incorruption, and this mortal shall have put on immortality, then shall be brought to pass the saying that is written, Death is swallowed up in victory. O death, where is thy sting? O grave, where is thy victory? The sting of death is sin; and the strength of sin is the law. But thanks be to God, which giveth us the victory through our Lord Jesus Christ.

2 Corinthians 5:8: We are confident, I say, and willing rather to be absent from the body, and to be present with the Lord.

ANIMALS SERVING GOD'S PURPOSE

There are many animals in the Bible, but the following table will name just a few that served God's specific purpose.

ANIMAL	WORKS	SCRIPTURE
Bears	Bears attacked the 42 children for insulting the great Prophet Elisha because of his bald head.	2 Kings 2:23-24
Dogs	Dogs licked up the blood of Ahab and ate the flesh of Jezebel.	1 Kings 21:19; 1 Kings 21:23-24; 1 Kings 22:38; 2 Kings 9:10; 2 Kings 36-37
Donkey	When Balaam tried to curse Israel, His donkey saw an angel and spoke out. Lost Asses caused Saul to find Samuel, who anointed him Israel's first King. A Jawbone of an Ass was used to kill a thousand men. Jesus rode into Jerusalem riding on a Donkey (colt).	Numbers 22:21-25 1 Samuel 9:3-27 1 Samuel 10:1-16 Judges 15:14-17 Matthew 21:1-11; Mark 11:1-11
Dove	Doves were released from the ark by Noah and brought confirmation that the flood had ended. Dove was given as a sign of the Holy Spirit at the baptism of Jesus.	Genesis 8:8-11 Matthew 3:16-17
Fish	Jonah was swallowed by a great fish which lead to him finally obeying God.	Jonah 1:17
Foxes	Samson used 300 Foxes to set the Philistines' fields on fire.	Judges 15:4-5

Frogs, gnats, flies, and locusts.	Moses had Aaron's staffs turned to snakes as a sign for Pharaoh, and God struck Egypt with plagues of frogs, gnats, flies, and locusts.	Exodus 8 and 10
Lions	In Canaan, God helped Samson kill a lion.	Judges 14:5-6
	When Daniel was thrown in the Lion's den, an angel protected Daniel by shutting up the Lion's mouth.	Daniel 6:22
Quails	In the desert, God provided the Israelites with quail to eat.	Numbers 11:31-33
Ram	For Abraham, a ram caught in the bush was God's substitute for the sacrifice of Isaac.	Genesis 22:13
Ravens	Ravens brought the prophet Elijah food during the drought.	1 Kings 17:4-6
Serpent	The Serpent was used in the Garden of Eden.	Genesis 3:1-5
	The Lord sent snakes to afflict the Israelites in the desert.	Numbers 21:6
Turtledoves and pigeons	Turtledoves and pigeons were used as animal sacrifices in the Old Testament.	Leviticus 1:14-17
Worms	The worms ate Jonah's shade tree.	Jonah 4:7

JEHOVAH-JIREH: THE LORD WILL PROVIDE
THE RAM (GEN. 22:13-14)

SIX STEPS TO SALVATION

ACKNOWLEDGE THAT YOU ARE A SINNER

✞ Romans 3:23-26: For all have sinned, and come short of the glory of God; Being justified freely by his grace through the redemption that is in Christ Jesus Whom God hath set forth to be a propitiation through faith in his blood, to declare his righteousness for the remission of sins that are past, through the forbearance of God; To declare, I say, at this time his righteousness: that he might be just, and the justifier of him which believeth in Jesus.

✞ Romans 6:23: For the wages of sin is death; but the gift of God is eternal life through Jesus Christ our Lord.

✞ Luke 18:13-14: And the publican, standing afar off, would not lift up so much as his eyes unto heaven, but smote upon his breast, saying, God be merciful to me a sinner. I tell you, this man went down to his house justified rather than the other: for every one that exalteth himself shall be abased; and he that humbleth himself shall be exalted.

REPENT OF YOUR SINS

✞ Acts 3:19: Repent ye therefore, and be converted, that your sins may be blotted out, when the times of refreshing shall come from the presence of the Lord.

✞ Luke 13:3: I tell you, Nay: but, except ye repent, ye shall all likewise perish.

✞ Matthew 4:17: From that time Jesus began to preach, and to say, Repent: for the kingdom of heaven is at hand.

CONFESS YOUR SINS

✞ 1 John 1:9-10: If we confess our sins, he is faithful and just to forgive us our sins, and to cleanse us from all unrighteousness. If we say that we have not sinned, we make him a liar, and his word is not in us.

✞ Romans 10:10-11: For with the heart man believeth unto righteousness; and with the mouth confession is made unto salvation. For the scripture saith, whosoever believeth on him shall not be ashamed.

✞ Psalms 32:5: I acknowledged my sin unto thee, and mine iniquity have I not hid. I said, I will confess my transgressions unto the Lord; and thou forgavest the iniquity of my sin.

FORSAKE YOUR SINFUL WAYS

✝ Isaiah 55:7: Let the wicked forsake his way, and the unrighteous man his thoughts: and let him return unto the Lord, and he will have mercy upon him; and to our God, for he will abundantly pardon.

BELIEVE IN JESUS CHRIST

✝ John 3:16-17: For God so loved the world, that he gave his only begotten Son, that whosoever believeth in him should not perish, but have everlasting life. For God sent not his Son into the world to condemn the world; but that the world through him might be saved.

✝ Romans 10:9: That if thou shalt confess with thy mouth the Lord Jesus, and shalt believe in thine heart that God hath raised him from the dead, thou shalt be saved.

RECEIVE

✝ John 1:11-12: He came unto his own, and his own received him not. But as many as received him, to them gave he power to become the sons of God, even to them that believe on his name.

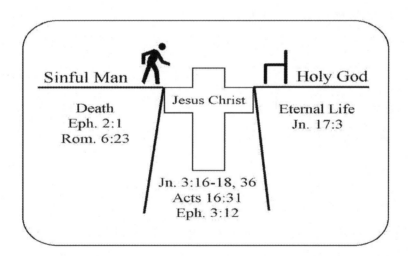

SAMPLE SINNERS PRAYER

LORD JESUS, I ACKNOWLEDGE THAT I AM A SINNER. FORGIVE ME OF MY SINS; CLEANSE MY THOUGHTS, WORDS, AND ACTIONS. I BELIEVE THAT YOU DIED FOR MY SINS AND ROSE FROM THE GRAVE. I ASK YOU IN NAME OF JESUS CHRIST TO SAVE ME AND CLEANSE ME OF ALL UNRIGHTEOUSNESS. I RECEIVE YOU INTO MY HEART AS MY LORD AND SAVIOR. IN JESUS NAME. AMEN!

CHRISTIAN "I AM" STATEMENTS

Authors Unknown
Copied from various Internet links in the public domain
Chart created and many statements added by: Author: Dreamer L. Brown

I am a child of the Most High God.	Romans 8:16
I am redeemed *"set free-rescued"* from the hands of the enemy.	Psalms 107:2
I am forgiven *"excused for all my faults"* by Christ Jesus.	Colossians 1:13-14
I am saved by grace *"God's unmerited favor"* through faith.	Ephesians 2:8
I am justified *"freed from guilt and shame".*	Romans 5:1
I am sanctified *"set apart and consecrated".*	I Corinthians 6:11
I am a new creature in Christ Jesus.	2 Corinthians 5:17
I am partaker of Jesus divine nature.	2 Peter 1:4
I am redeemed from the curse of the law.	Galatians 3:13
I am delivered from the powers of darkness.	Colossians 1:13
I am led by the Spirit of God.	Romans 8:14
I am a son of God.	Romans 8:14
I am kept in safety wherever I go.	Psalms 91:11
I am getting all my needs met by Jesus Christ.	Philippians 4:19
I am casting all my cares upon Jesus.	I Peter 5:7
I am strong in the Lord and in the power of His might.	Ephesians 6:10
I am doing all things through Christ who strengthens me.	Philippians 4:13
I am an heir with God and a joint heir with Christ Jesus.	Romans 8:17
I am heir to the blessings of Abraham.	Galatians 3:13-14
I am blessed coming in and blessed going out.	Deuteronomy 26:6-10
I am an heir of eternal life.	I John 5:11-12
I am healed by His stripes.	I Peter 2:24
I am above and not beneath.	Deuteronomy 28:13

I am more than a conqueror "one who succeeds."	Romans 8:37
I am establishing God's Word here on earth.	Matthew 16:19
I am an over comer.	Revelation 12:11
I am walking by faith and not by sight.	2 Corinthians 5:7
I am casting down every vain imagination.	2 Corinthians 10:4-5
I am bringing every thought into captivity.	2 Corinthians 10:5
I am being transformed "changed" by the renewing of my mind.	Romans 12:1-2
I am a laborer together with Christ.	I Corinthians 3:9
I am the righteousness of God.	2 Corinthians 5:21
I am an imitator of Jesus Christ.	Ephesians 5:1
I am the light of the world.	Matthew 5:14
I am the salt of the earth.	Matthew 5:13
I am a fisher of men.	Matthew 4:18
I am chosen by God.	Matthew 22:14
I am a peculiar person and from the royal priesthood.	1 Peter 2:9
I am an Ambassador "a diplomatic official of the highest rank appointed as a representative" for Christ.	2 Corinthians 5:20
I am dressed for spiritual warfare.	Ephesians 6:11-18
I am empowered to take authority over demonic forces.	Luke 10:19

FOUNDATION OF THE WORD

This course and all Bible study courses by Dr. Dreamer L. Brown are suitable for beginner, intermediate and advanced Bible Study.

CONSULTANT SERVICES

Teaching the material from this booklet is offered at local churches and schools for a nominal registration fee per student plus the cost of each booklet. You may inquire more on this offering by contacting Dr. Dreamer L. Brown at the address on the following page or at email address: willdream2@aol.com.

DISTANCE LEARNING CERTIFICATES

The Distance learning course is for those who prefer "home studies" instead of classroom studies. After completing the course, simply return the entire booklet to CDM, Inc. for review and grading. After checking your answers we will return your booklet and send a certificate of completion. The distance learning registration fee is in addition to the cost of the booklet and must be paid in advance of receiving the certificate of completion and grading. You may inquire more on this offering by contacting Dr. Dreamer L. Brown at email address: willdream2@aol.com.

Please print your name and title as you want it printed on your certificate of completion:

_____

PERSONALIZED WORKBOOKS

CDM, Inc. will create personalized workbooks with other Bible translations and eliminate or add pages to create a customized booklet for churches and schools. There is a one time up-front fee for the customized manual. Following the customization, the book will be published and individual copies may be purchased at the said rate per student manual with a minimum guarantee of books. Inquire more on this offering.

FOUNDATION OF THE WORD
ORDER FORM

Name _____

Organization _____

Address _____

_____

Number of Copies _____

SEVERAL OPTIONS TO ORDER BOOKS:

1. MAIL ORDER FORM TO P.O. BOX
2. EMAIL ORDER TO: WILLDREAM2@AOL.COM
3. FAX ORDER SHEET: 609-723-2637
4. ORDER ONLINE: WWW.TRAFFORD.COM

Teacher's edition with the answers is available for a nominal fee. Inquire more on this offering.

Make Check or Money Order Payable to
Dreamer L. Brown

SEND $19.95 PER BOOKLET TO:

Dr. Dreamer L. Brown
CDM, Inc.
P.O. Box 151
Wrightstown, N.J. 08562

OTHER BOOKS BY AUTHOR

PREPARE FOR THE BATTLEFIELD: AUTHOR: DREAMER L. BROWN, Ph.D

Search the scriptures for yourself and become a weapon against the enemy through spiritual warfare. Becoming a Christian is like joining the army. You declare your faithfulness to Jesus Christ and your readiness to serve him. Then you begin a lifetime of spiritual training and combat. Christians are Soldiers, equipped with weapons; and the power to bind and loose. The Christian life is not a playground. It is a front line battlefield. Look for this book at your local bookstore.

SOUL PATROL: AUTHOR: DREAMER L. BROWN, Ph.D

Soul Patrol is committed to teaching the fundamental principles of God's Word and dedicated to making resources available that will help equip you for evangelism. In order for us to be effective in evangelism, we must first understand the five-fold ministry given to the Church. The Lord has equipped the Church but we need to know those that labor among us and understand their ministry call. Everyone should witness for the Lord, but the Evangelist should be in the forefront with evangelism. In order to establish a "soul winning" growth in the church, leaders must acknowledge the evangelist as an integral part of the five-fold Body of Christ and empower them to use their gifts of evangelism. Regardless of our calling in ministry, we can learn from each other. We all have different gifts but when the five-fold ministry work together and every joint in the body fulfill its responsibility then we can effectively get the job done. Soul Patrol will provide you with the essential building blocks for a richer walk with God, and motivate you for Kingdom Building. Read this book and ignite your passion to reach those who do not know Christ. Gain spiritual understanding and discover a new dimension of Spirit-led evangelism. Soul Patrol is designed to teach new converts as well as seasoned Believers how to go out and spread the good news about Jesus Christ. This book can be used for individual or group study. Many people are looking for a church that's alive evangelistically. Growing churches put the work of evangelism first into the hands of the Evangelist and then empower the entire congregation to evangelize. The mission field is in our own neighborhoods, workplaces, schools, and within our extended families. We pray that God will use you in a mighty way to go and compel the lost to accept the Lord Jesus Christ. Look for this book at your local bookstore.

Printed in the United States
By Bookmasters